Bitcoin: The Honest Money

Bitcoin:
The Honest Money

Alex von Frankenberg, Ph.D.

Bitcoin Magazine Books
Nashville, TN

Bitcoin: The Honest Money by Alex von Frankenberg, Ph.D.

This work is the English-language translation of *Das ehrliche Geld*, first published in German in 2025 by Aprycot Media. The English edition is published by arrangement with the author.

ISBN 979-8-9999542-6-8 (Paperback)

ISBN 979-8-9999542-8-2 (eBook)

Published by Bitcoin Magazine Books
An imprint of BTC Inc.
6339 Charlotte Pike, Unit #B321, Nashville TN, 37209
Address all queries to contact@btcmedia.org

Interior design by MediaNeighbours.com

Contents

Dedicated to an honest, fair, democratic, and free society.

Thank you,

Satoshi Nakamoto,

For truly changing the world.

You deserve the Nobel Prize for Economics. And Peace.

And a very special thank you to

Jan Goslicki and Jörg v. Minckwitz,

who showed me the way to Bitcoin.

And THANK YOU to the wonderful Bitcoin community.

I would especially like to thank my dear wife, Natalie.

She tolerated and supported my Bitcoin journey

and gave me the energy and time to write this book.

WARNING:

READING THIS BOOK COULD LEAD
TO SIGNIFICANT AND UNCONTROLLABLE
BITCOIN PURCHASES

= 2€
= 4€
= 6€
2€

A Little Story About Inflation

When I was a teenager, I delivered newspapers. I earned 10 German marks (DM) per hour. That was enough money to buy 33 scoops of ice cream, since a single scoop only cost 30 cents, or pfennig, as they were back then.

Fast forward to 2025: today, a teenager delivering newspapers earns at most €12 per hour. However, a scoop of ice cream now costs a hefty €1.50, and sometimes more than €2 in the big cities. This means that for every hour of newspaper delivery, you can afford at best a mere eight scoops of ice cream, but it's often less than that.

The working time of a newspaper boy or girl has been significantly devalued in Germany over the last forty years. An hour's work now yields only six to eight scoops of ice cream, compared with the 33 scoops it originally earned in the 1980s. That's a loss of around 80%.

If I had put my 10 DM in a drawer, found them forty years later, and exchanged them for €5, I'd only get about two to three scoops of ice cream—a loss of over 90%.

This concerns inflation and its redistributive effects. It's not only saved money that's devalued; it's also the time that's spent earning that money—or to be more precise, earning a fixed basket of goods. As money loses value, so does the actual time we spent earning it. On average, we receive far less in real goods for the work we do.

Inflation, the continual devaluation of money, is a huge problem. The global money supply (M2) is estimated at around $120 trillion (see Figure 4). Even at an inflation rate of 4% (and the global rate is likely higher), the M2 of approximately $120 trillion implies that $4.8 trillion in purchasing power is destroyed each year. That's more than the entire gross national product of Germany.[1] Inflation affects billions of people. Almost everyone, in fact. And the less you earn, the more you are dispossessed by inflation. The vast majority of people, which I estimate at around 90% of all citizens, have no way to avoid the devaluation of money. They lose out as their savings are devalued, and their wages fail to keep pace with rising inflation.

Major historical upheavals and revolutions have very often been preceded by inflation, for example, the French Revolution. Currency devaluation also played a significant role in the collapse of the Western Roman Empire in AD 476, some one thousand years before the collapse of the Eastern Roman Empire. Therefore, inflation also represents a serious threat to democratic societies today.

The amount of bitcoin will not increase in the long term. There will never be more than 21 million bitcoin, and no one will ever be able to change that. At this point in early 2026, there are already 19.9 million bitcoin, a good 95% of the set amount. This means that any remaining expansion (or new issuance) of bitcoin will amount to just under 5%; not in the next year, but over approximately one hundred fifteen years. Around the year 2140, 100% of all bitcoin will have been mined, and there will simply not be any more. This means that the share of money you hold in bitcoin will not be devalued against a basket of goods over a decade or even a century. Your share won't be diluted. Bitcoin does not inflate; when measured in bitcoin, goods actually become cheaper over time. So the money you exchange for bitcoin today will buy you at least as many scoops of ice cream in ten years as it does now—and probably more. A lot more. This is the fundamental essence of bitcoin.

21 Chapters

This book comprises twenty-one chapters, grouped into six sections, that explore the benefits, characteristics, effects, unique features, growing adoption, and long-term impact of Bitcoin.

Using simple examples and anecdotes, the book aims to explain what Bitcoin is, why it can be beneficial for individuals, societies, and the planet, its unique features and drawbacks, the current state of adoption, and the long-term effect it can—and likely will—have.

Section 1 is about inflation and bitcoin's use as a store of value. Due to its properties, bitcoin is the most suitable means of preserving value in the long term. At the same time, inflation—and especially the nearly complete devaluation of money over the long run—is one of the biggest monetary problems of our time. Bitcoin enables the transfer of value to be conducted very easily and very inexpensively, both globally and over time. No other currency preserves value for even thirty years; over a period of one hundred years, virtually all currencies lose more than 90% of their value. At least 90% of people are adversely affected by inflation. There are very few winners.

Section 2 presents the second major use case of bitcoin. It enables value to be held outside of the mainstream financial system, thus protecting it from confiscation through bail-ins or government intervention. This requires you to keep your bitcoin in your own possession rather than storing it in a bank or an exchange.

Section 3 describes Bitcoin adoption processes. Network effects could lead bitcoin to becoming the de facto standard for storing value. Much like Microsoft Windows became the de facto standard for PC operating systems, bitcoin could also become the preferred medium for value storage and other applications outside of the crypto world. This process would likely promote substantial value appreciation.

Section 4 examines the origins and technical features of Bitcoin. Bitcoin can be compared to the internet as we know it and is often referred to as the *Internet of Value.*

Section 5 addresses some commonly cited drawbacks. Many people are deterred by short-term price fluctuations, while others are bothered by the high energy consumption or even the lack of a centralized authority governing Bitcoin.

Section 6 discusses personal and societal effects. *You don't change Bitcoin; Bitcoin changes you* is often quoted as the effect Bitcoin adoption has on Bitcoiners.

The book concludes by underscoring its central thesis: Bitcoin is honest money.

It is quite possible that Bitcoin and its underlying technology will change our world more profoundly than many other major technologies have so far, including the computer, the internet, artificial intelligence, or even certain biotechnologies.

It is also possible that Bitcoin could fail, though, in my opinion, that's highly unlikely.

Should Bitcoin prove to be a truly world-changing technology, it will most benefit those of us who come to grips with it and join in early. Maybe this is where this book can help.

Introduction:
What Is Bitcoin?

Bitcoin is, first and foremost, a technology. First introduced seventeen years ago with the launch of the Bitcoin blockchain on January 3, 2009, Bitcoin remains a relatively young and unestablished technology.

What makes Bitcoin special are its unique features. It is much like fire in the Stone Age. Once humans discovered how to use fire, the world was a different place. Our evolution, and even the development of our brains and intelligence, was significantly influenced by our discovery and control of fire. We suddenly learned to cook meat, warm our caves, and shine bright light into the darkness. Nothing like it had happened to us before. Just as new and unique were the inventions of the wheel, the printing press, the computer, the internet, and much more.

So what makes Bitcoin so special?

In stark contrast to the printing press and the internet, which have both made it possible to copy and widely distribute information at will, Bitcoin is the very first technology that makes it impossible to copy and thus duplicate the data associated with its network. This is very important because that data represents money. And when anyone—or even just a few entities operating at scale, such as central banks—can create money at will, that money won't hold its value for long.

The digital asset, bitcoin, cannot be copied. It can be either here or there—never in two places at once. That is something entirely new. Information has always been easy to duplicate digitally, and once shared, it cannot be undone (except in the rarest cases where every single copy is destroyed). This cannot occur with Bitcoin; this unique property is called *digital scarcity.*

There are more special features. Bitcoin is open source, meaning its software is transparent, accessible, and publicly visible. With a little programming knowledge, you can see exactly what the software does. This makes Bitcoin not only transparent but also honest. It functions exactly as presented in the software. There are no tricks and no backdoors.

Another crucial feature here is that no one—no individual, no group, not even a state—can control or arbitrarily change the Bitcoin technology. That has far-reaching implications. Nobody can manipulate the technology for their own benefit. A complex process of consensus and acceptance among the parties involved in Bitcoin prevents unwanted changes; any relevant updates to the software are made only every few years.

Bitcoin is a new kind of database, but unlike previous databases, the Bitcoin database—the blockchain—is distributed and decentralized. New entries in it are bundled into *blocks* and added according to specific rules. This process of adding to and modifying the database is carried out not by a central authority but rather through decentralized competition among *miners*. Ultimately, chance decides which miner gets the opportunity to add the next block to the blockchain. Many copies of this database are also verified and stored in multiple locations. Thousands of *nodes* perform this task, thereby ensuring that the blockchain adheres to the agreed-upon rules.

The result is that there is no central control over the database, a crucial and novel feature of Bitcoin. No one can simply change the rules; therefore, no one can alter the maximum number of 21 million bitcoin. No matter how urgent the problem, no matter how great the supposed crisis, no one can simply turn 21 million bitcoin into 22 million. This means that bitcoin is a finite, non-reproducible asset that is inherently immune to inflation. This is its fourth key property, and it is unique.

Together, these essential features enable a particular (but not exclusive) application: digital money that no one controls, cannot be arbitrarily changed, and most importantly, cannot be inflated. Money that is fully transparent, easily digitally transferable worldwide at very low cost, and particularly well-suited not only as a store of value but also as a medium of exchange, and much more. Transfers occur directly from person to person. All you need is access to the Bitcoin blockchain; no banks or central banks are required. It is like cash, but without intermediaries—a bit like gold, only digital. Once a bitcoin (which exists only as information) has been transferred, the sender no longer has access to it; only the recipient has.

In the last fifty years, digitalization has fundamentally changed our world. Computers and the internet have enabled instantaneous, global access to a vast amount of information. Digital twins of machines allow for the optimization of their design and operation, and artificial intelligence is beginning to surpass human capabilities in many areas. In a sense, this is digitizing the human being, or more specifically, the intelligence that until now has been bound within the physical brain.

It seems likely that Bitcoin will have a world-changing impact, comparable to, or even greater than, that of the computer, the internet, the smartphone, and other digital technologies. If Bitcoin can curb or even prevent the negative consequences of massive, ongoing global inflation, it could significantly change the world.

Banks, central banks, and governments, however, have mastered this alchemy of money. Decoupled from gold and centrally controlled, money can be artificially multiplied, printed, or, as the saying goes, created out of thin air. The creation of money occurs when central banks buy outstanding sovereign bonds, for example, or when banks grant loans. When a bank provides financing to a homebuyer, the new loan funds are created out of nothing. New digital money comes into being; colloquially, the bank has printed money. The same occurs when a central bank purchases a bond. It simply creates new money to finance it.

With bitcoin, money that was once tied to physical objects, like gold or paper currency, or was centrally controlled and alterable in digital form by banks or central banks, suddenly becomes independent and decentralized. Countless attempts to artificially create gold have failed. In this sense, bitcoin is a bit like gold; it cannot be artificially multiplied. Unlike gold, however, it can be transferred globally in seconds. And it's not possible to simply *find* more of this gold. The number of bitcoin that will ever exist has been predetermined. Bitcoin is digital; you might even call it digital gold.

Bitcoin is not a technology that marginally improves what already exists. It is, however, a technology that may fundamentally transform many things—a completely new, disruptive technology. The difficult thing about disruptive technologies is recognizing them as such. There are many well-known examples of highly intelligent and renowned individuals who failed to recognize disruptive technologies for what they were. Early on, many *experts* vastly underestimated the possible success of the internet.

Two years after the launch of the iPhone, Nokia was the undisputed market leader with a global market share of around 40%. Just like the Apple Macintosh, Nokia expected the iPhone to remain a niche product. The phone had a large screen, few physical buttons, and a battery life of only a few hours, whereas some Nokia models could operate for several days without recharging, whereas some Nokia models could operate for several days without recharging. Some five years after the iPhone launched, Nokia's mobile division was finished following an ill-fated acquisition by Microsoft.

My method for recognizing disruptive innovations is almost instinctive. It is the immediate, unfiltered thought, the gut reaction that goes, *What a bunch of nonsense.* Always, and I mean always, when you think this, there are exactly two possibilities. Either it really is nonsense, or it is a completely novel, world-changing innovation that you simply do not understand or cannot conceive of, and therefore initially consider it to be nonsense. The art is in distinguishing nonsense from the nonsensical, i.e., foolishness from mind-blowing, world-changing innovation. This is extremely difficult. After all, a great many innovations, especially some of the big ones, do fail and become—in hindsight—simply nonsense.

The path to understanding involves examining the technology's specific features in relation to the market. What new applications do they enable that did not exist before? What insurmountable problems could they solve? Do they make the previously unimaginable possible? Can they do all this without great cost?

The significance and impact of disruptive technologies are inherently difficult to understand. Their mechanisms are often complex, initially unrefined, inaccessible, and cumbersome to use; as prototypes, they function poorly at best. On top of that, they often target markets that do not (yet) exist with products that have never been seen before. Everything is new: the technology, products, markets, business models, partner ecosystems, suppliers, distributors, and much more. Only a small number of entrepreneurs ultimately succeed in recognizing these barriers and still implement their ideas. We know the big names like Steve Jobs, Elon Musk, Bill Gates, and Jeff Bezos. But we do not know the countless others who gave up or failed.

What makes it even harder is that we are almost always wrong at some point in the process. When new technologies fail, we have been wrong in initially overestimating them. Similarly, when new technologies succeed, we are wrong again, this time in underestimating their success and potential, especially at the beginning. We are rarely able to anticipate the magnitude of success of a completely new disruptive technology. Almost always, we underestimate its success—often by orders of magnitude. Or who would have thought that Apple, worth $6 billion in 2001, would be valued at around $4 trillion more than twenty years later in 2025?

Disruptive innovations are complex. Their significance and impact are difficult to grasp, and they often have a ripple effect across multiple areas. This means our only option is to approach them systematically. Many small steps, sometimes big ones. Some fast, some slow.

To summarize, disruptive technologies are hard to recognize. We regularly dismiss them as nonsense, and we are nearly always wrong in assessing their impact because we tend to underestimate them. Furthermore, we can only make sense of them step by step.

Yet here is what I propose: Bitcoin is one of the most disruptive technologies we will see in our lifetime. Do you think Bitcoin is nonsense? That's perfectly fine. Do you believe that Bitcoin will have no greater impact than the fax machine did? Welcome to the club. That's just how I felt at the beginning.

Why is Bitcoin so disruptive? As mentioned, this technology enables digital scarcity for the first time in human history—digital goods that cannot be copied. Bitcoin's disruption lies in its permanently limited supply, because conventional, arbitrarily expandable money leads to many enormous problems, including often uncontrolled and ultimately inefficient government spending; wealth redistribution from the poor to the rich; short-term overconsumption that causes significant environmental damage; short-term thinking; consumption over capital accumulation; and much more. The multiplication of money also makes it much easier to finance wars.

In the end, it's quite simple: bitcoin cannot be expanded beyond 21 million units. The radical expansion of the money supply, i.e., the physical and digital issuance of new money, devalues existing money and, with it, the work and time required to acquire the same basket of goods. With bitcoin, an expansion of the money supply is simply impossible; therefore, the basket of goods, when measured in bitcoin, becomes increasingly cheap over the decades. This is quite different from state-backed currencies like the euro or the dollar, where your money buys you fewer and fewer scoops of ice cream as time goes by.

Section 1:
Inflation

Inflation is difficult to grasp.

The commonly accepted definition of inflation is the increase in the price of a typical consumer basket of goods. This basket is defined by the Federal Statistical Office of Germany and adjusted every five years according to changes in consumer behavior. The price increases measured in this basket are then referred to as inflation.

Not every price increase reflects inflation. Price increases can be temporary. For example, a poor harvest may drive up the price of potatoes, but the following year, if the harvest is good, prices may fall again. The price increase in the first year would be offset by the subsequent decrease in the following year; in other words, there would be no permanent inflation.

The Austrian School of Economics defines inflation as an expansion of the money supply. However, more money does not always lead to price increases, especially not in the short term. If the newly created money remains in bank accounts and is not spent, prices do not rise. Even if the new money is spent, it is not always reflected in the officially measured inflation rate when it is used on goods not included in the consumer price index.

For example, when stocks or real estate are purchased, it is asset price inflation and does not affect the prices of consumer goods. Similarly, if newly created money leads to price increases that are offset by higher productivity, there may still be no measurable inflation. In short, more money does not necessarily lead to an increase in officially measured inflation. Because multiple factors are at play, the causes of inflation are not always clear. It may be driven by an increase in the money supply, the scarcity of individual goods, people's willingness to spend or save, changes in productivity, or some combination of these factors.

Ultimately, this is also irrelevant because we know that the purchasing power of money always decreases over long periods of time. This was true even two thousand years ago in ancient Rome. And we know that, in the long run, there is always more money. Price increases erode not only the purchasing power of money but also the productivity gains that should otherwise lead to falling prices. If a fisherman now catches nine fish in eight hours of work instead of eight fish, and thus becomes more productive, a fish no longer costs him one hour of work, but only fifty-three minutes. The price of a fish, measured in working time, falls when he catches more fish. The ice cream example above shows how the price of ice cream scoops, measured in the newspaper boy's work time, has increased over time.

In the long run, the correlation remains true. Adding more money devalues its purchasing power, whereas other factors that drive price increases play a minor role over extended periods. The decisive factor is the money supply.

Chapter 1:
Over Time, Money Loses Its Value

In 1979, when I was about thirteen years old—at the height of the seventies' inflation—my mother and I were standing at the checkout counter. My parents had just separated. Money was tight, and rapidly rising prices were exacerbating the situation. It was so tight, in fact, that my mother couldn't pay for all the groceries, and we had to put a few things back. The situation at the checkout counter was not only embarrassing and painful but also one of the most powerful motivating factors in my life, prompting me, for many years thereafter, to focus fully on my education and work hard. I've never forgotten that incident to this day.

In 2016, I took my family on vacation to Italy. Completely out of the blue, our daughter, who was thirteen at the time, asked, "Papa, why isn't more money printed for kids who are poor or sick?" Just like that. Although I am sure we had discussed various financial crises from time to time, including the *whatever-it-takes* strategy of Mario Draghi, who was then the President of the European Central Bank, the ECB's monetary policy was not really something we discussed as a family. I was stunned by what my daughter said. Printing money as a solution to all sorts of problems was the explicit strategy of central banks and politicians, and now this idea had seeped, subconsciously, into the general population. Now, even children saw that printing money was a better solution than saving it. If money were needed for poor or sick kids, why not simply print it? At the time, our daughter did not think to ask whether the required funds could be generated by cutting costs elsewhere.

Governments continually face additional responsibilities related to infrastructure, education, population demographics, domestic and foreign security, among others. To manage these unbudgeted demands, a government needs money. It could cut spending in another area or increase revenue through more taxes and levies. Both approaches are unpopular. It is much easier and faster to quietly print more money. This is the process when a government creates new debt and the central bank or commercial banks buy government bonds. New credit increases the money supply, but the more money there is in circulation, the more likely it is that prices will rise if the supply of goods remains the same.

On August 18, 2022, Isabel Schnabel (who graduated at the top of her class in economics at Mannheim, was a professor of economics in Bonn, Germany, and now sits on the Executive Board of the ECB) gave a lecture at the Chamber of Commerce and Industry in Bonn. While explaining the causes of inflation, she stated that, in the ECB's models, the money supply no longer played a role. Inflation, she said, had other causes, including supply chain disruptions, the war in Ukraine, energy prices, collective bargaining agreements, and high corporate profits.

The money supply does, in fact, affect prices, and numerous economic models show how. But let's take a look at a simple hypothetical example. Consider the city of Cologne, with a population of approximately one million. Imagine if everyone were suddenly given €100 million, deposited into their bank accounts. What would happen? On the first day, nothing would happen. Everyone would probably just marvel at their newfound wealth. Then they go out to celebrate. On the second day, the first bars run dry, and the same happens again on the third and fourth days. I would argue that no prices would rise in the first week. After a week, though, the first bar owners would raise their prices. By the second week, more would follow suit. Now, when do Cologne's real estate prices start rising? Suppose that after about four weeks, the first newly rich Cologne citizen purchases an apartment. Then the next, and the next. After about two months, real estate prices inevitably begin to climb.

The point is, the increased money supply has a delayed effect. It takes some time for new money to circulate, and then a little more time for prices to rise. In our fictional example, it takes a week for Cologne's bars to raise beer prices, and two months to observe the effect of new money on real estate prices. In complex economies, it may take a few years for prices to rise after the money supply increases. But the effect is obvious. More money spent on the same quantity of goods leads to higher prices. The supply, whether it be beer or apartments, will increase over time, but only gradually. When a short-term increase in demand meets an initially constant supply, the result, of course, is that prices will rise. If the newly rich people of Cologne only spend their wealth on beer and apartments, the prices of other goods do not change. If beer and housing are excluded from the official inflation basket, measured inflation will rise only slightly, if at all. Yet an increasing money supply will still lead to rising prices.

What exactly is the effect of inflation?

There's a simple and fairly accurate formula that estimates how long it takes for inflation to halve the value of money. Seventy divided by the inflation rate equals the number of years until the value of money is halved. For example, at an inflation rate of 2%, the value of money is halved in thirty-five years (70 divided by 2). At a 7% inflation rate, it takes only ten years to halve the value. Over the course of three decades at 7% inflation, money's value is cut in half three times. That means the purchasing power of €10 first becomes €5 (first halving), then €2.50 (second halving), then €1.25 (third halving). In other words, at the end of thirty years with an inflation rate of 7% per year, you will have lost almost 90% of your money's value or purchasing power. That is a very big loss.

Halving the purchasing power means that, on average, everything will cost twice as much. Put it another way, if prices stayed the same, it would be equivalent to your account balance and salary being cut in half. So if you had €1,000 in savings, you'd effectively be left with €500 if the value of money was halved and prices remained constant.

The European Central Bank defines price stability as 2% inflation, but this is a contradiction in terms. Money that halves in value over thirty-five years is not stable. Moreover, the euro doesn't decline by 2% per year; the rate of decline varies substantially. So, 2% is merely a target, a desired average at best. It would be a considerable stretch of the imagination to call the euro's monetary value *stable*.

Why is inflation unfair?

If someone benefits from an increase in wealth while the supply of goods remains temporarily constant, then someone else is disadvantaged. If one person has more money and therefore can buy more, someone else will be buying less. Price increases are the market's mechanism for balancing this out. Wealth cannot be created through printing money or through inflation itself. Instead, wealth is created by producing more goods—which occurs either through more work being done or through higher productivity. Having more money simply redistributes those goods differently, giving them to those who receive the new money first and taking them away from those who receive it later or never at all.

The Cantillon effect posits that newly created money is distributed unevenly. Some get it first, some later, and some never do. Those who receive newly created money can purchase more goods with it, thereby making those goods no longer available to others. The market then regulates the *distribution* of the remaining goods via rising prices.[2]

It has to be this way. If everyone worked the same amount and produced the same amount of goods, but some were then suddenly able to buy more, the others must be able to buy less. When additional money provides some people with access to goods and services, those goods and services will be in short supply elsewhere.

So, increasing the money supply (otherwise known as printing money) redistributes that money and with it the claim to goods. From a societal or political perspective, there may be good reasons for this. Ultimately, the increased money supply and resulting inflation take from some and give to others.

Inflation is unfair and socially unjust, but above all, it is dishonest. Unfair, because just like that and for no apparent reason, some people can suddenly afford less. Socially unjust, because the lower end of the income ladder is typically hit the hardest. Dishonest, because the true causes of inflation are left unspoken, while less relevant causes, for example, the war in Ukraine, greedy corporations, and foreign countries imposing tariffs, serve as scapegoats. And above all, dishonest, because we are constantly told that inflation benefits us. We are told that without inflation, everyone would be worse off and the economy would collapse.

Inflation and currency devaluation lead to unconscious and dishonest redistribution, ultimately from the less affluent to the wealthy and to the government. The government benefits through a few mechanisms. As wages rise due to inflation, taxes also rise. And thanks to progressive tax brackets, where higher incomes are subject to even higher tax rates, taxes rise disproportionately. The same applies to capital gains from the sale of assets that have risen in price.

For example, if stock prices keep pace with inflation, you would actually lose money after selling up and paying taxes on the gains. The flip side is that debt shrinks. Nominally, it stays the same, but it's easier to repay with devalued money.

What's so bad about inflation?

Wages rise, too, people say.

Employees with strong bargaining power can negotiate wage increases that compensate for the devaluation of money. Most employees, however, do not have this kind of bargaining power. Most wage increases typically fall short of inflation. Even if wages were raised to keep pace with inflation, employees would still experience a loss of purchasing power because prices continue to rise throughout the year. Even with a cost-of-living adjustment at the end of the year, employees have been able to buy less and less each month for the previous twelve months. To fully compensate for the devaluation of money, year-end wage increases would have to exceed the rate of inflation.

Savings are hit even harder. Bank interest rates (as well as those on life insurance policies and savings accounts) are regularly below the inflation rate. For years, real interest rates on bank deposits in Germany have been negative—that is, interest rates on all forms of savings have lagged inflation. This is how savings are eroded.

Of course, you could invest your money more wisely than just putting it in a savings account. Over the long term, real estate, stocks, gold, and, of course, bitcoin all offer inflation-beating returns. The problem is, we just don't do it. In August 2024, private bank deposits in Germany amounted to almost €2.9 trillion. For example, a negative real interest rate (i.e., when the rate of inflation exceeds the nominal interest rate) of 4% implies more than €100 billion in annual loss of purchasing power. And for those who invest in stocks, many still make basic mistakes, such as selling in response to price declines or concentrating on a single area rather than diversifying. These individuals may also experience returns that fail to keep pace with inflation.

I don't have any detailed studies on this, but I would argue that a good 80–90% of Germans do not manage to offset inflation with their investments. Most people leave their money in the bank, allowing it to lose value year after year due to inflation.

So how high is inflation, really?

There are many perspectives on how to measure inflation. The most common is to measure the change in price of a typical basket of goods. However, this basket of goods may not accurately reflect the actual rate of inflation for several reasons. For one, it might not reflect what people are actually buying. Those real purchases could be experiencing different, and perhaps higher, price increases than the items in the measured basket. Furthermore, the way inflation is calculated treats quality improvements as price reductions, whereas deterioration in quality is hardly considered at all.

The Austrian School of Economics measures inflation by the expansion of the money supply. Regardless of how the money is used—whether for everyday purchases or investments—the more money available for a fixed supply of goods, the higher the prices. This view considers all goods in an economy, from daily necessities to stocks and real estate. In the eurozone, the M2 money supply has grown about 5.1% per year since the introduction of the euro on January 1, 2002. From early 2002 until the beginning of 2023, according to official statistics from the German Bundesbank, the money supply roughly tripled, rising from €4.9 trillion to €15.1 trillion. Since then, growth has slowed somewhat. This means that the expansion of the money supply is significantly greater than the increase in consumer prices, which is commonly referred to as inflation. The inflation, meaning in this case the additional money, didn't just show up in everyday goods like bread, milk, and eggs; it also flowed into real estate and stocks. This explains why it's becoming increasingly difficult for average earners to afford to buy homes. Increases in house prices are outpacing wage growth, as measured by the Consumer Price Index.[3]

When additional money drives up the prices of houses, gold, or stocks, this is only partially considered (if at all) in the measurement of inflation. But if incomes rise more slowly than real estate prices, money is devalued relative to real estate. You have to be in the workforce for longer to be able to buy a home. This is illustrated in the following chart, which shows the number of years of average U.S. wages required to purchase an average house in America.

Figure 1 (p. 14): Number of average annual incomes required to buy an average house in the U.S.

How long does it take to save for a house?

Years of Saving an Average Income Required to Buy an Average House

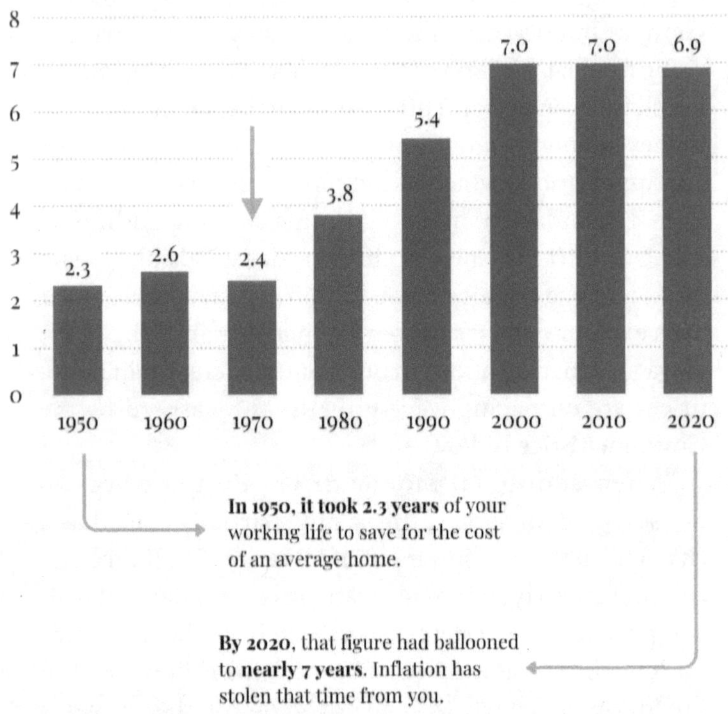

Source: FRED; thepeopleshistory.com; Mark Moss

When reported inflation statistics fail to capture certain price increases, major distortions occur. Real wages fall when nominal wage increases are tied to reported inflation. Returns on assets appear higher than they actually are. When nominal gains are taxed, the real value of your wealth is reduced if net returns (after tax) fall short of actual inflation. Anyone who can't secure a wage increase that outpaces actual inflation earns less in real terms.

Why might inflation remain perpetually high?

The sharp rise in energy prices and the supply chain problems of recent years may indeed be temporary. It's unlikely that gas and oil prices will increase by 10% every year. In fact, by August 2023, oil and gas prices in Germany had already fallen below pre-Ukraine-war levels.

Nevertheless, recent high price increases could continue from two perspectives. First, there are numerous factors that have a permanent inflationary effect. Second, a self-reinforcing loop can be set in motion that forces governments, through debt, or central banks, through bond purchases, to continue creating more and more money.

What are the reasons and factors that can lead to continued inflation?

Demographics: In many countries worldwide, populations are aging. Outside Africa as a whole, there are few countries where the population is growing. Germany's baby boom after the Second World War was followed by the well-known *Pillenknick*, a sharp decline in birth rates brought about by the introduction of the contraceptive pill. The first year with more than one million births in Germany was

1959, and the last was 1971. As these generations begin to retire and far fewer new workers enter the workforce, there is a shortage not only of labor but also of skilled workers. At the same time, the younger generation's mindset has changed: a good work-life balance is far more important today than it was for previous generations. Many are opting for part-time work and prioritizing family commitments over working overtime and pursuing a career. This leads to a significantly reduced labor supply and working hours, which in turn push wages up, raise costs, and add to price pressures. Meanwhile, the baby boomers are not yet exiting the consumer market.

Today, there is already a huge gap in the German pension system: in 2024, around €140 billion was paid into the pension fund from the federal budget. And as more baby boomers retire, the gap in the pension system will only grow larger. There are also substantial gaps in the pension system for civil servants, which is financed entirely by the state budget. Without spending cuts elsewhere or highly unpopular tax hikes, additional spending will have to be financed through new debt, which means creating more money.

The following chart shows the *cash flow* by age in Austria, which is likely comparable to figures in Germany and other countries. From childhood until you start work, money is transferred from the state to the citizen. As a working adult, you pay into society through taxes and other contributions. In old age, pension and medical costs again create negative cash flow, with society paying out to the elderly. If the entire population now lives longer, it is clear that society as a whole will experience negative cash flow. And to the extent that these costs are financed by printing money, additional inflation is created, at least in the long term.

FIGURE 2 (p. 18): Transfer payments and contributions of an average citizen to society over a lifetime

Deglobalization: Supply chain disruptions during the COVID-19 crisis, attacks on shipping routes by Houthi rebels, customs barriers, and growing awareness of environmental damage and the rise in CO_2 emissions from global trade are all contributing to greater local production. When cost savings from global production are no longer available, costs rise, and so do prices. Moreover, the increasingly critical stance toward China, Germany's most important trading partner, could further erode the cost and productivity benefits Germany has long enjoyed if trade with China were restricted.

Energy transition: When sufficient capacity has been built to supply all of Germany with renewable energy, energy production may be relatively inexpensive. The wind that powers turbines costs nothing, after all. However, the path to get there is long and expensive. Bureaucracy, in particular, is preventing the rapid expansion of renewable energy, and significant excess capacity must be created to ensure the security of supply when the sun isn't shining and the wind isn't blowing. This goes hand in hand with a heavy dependence on scarce rare earth metals. Over 90% of solar

Cash Flow Between a Citizen and Society

In Austria, 2015

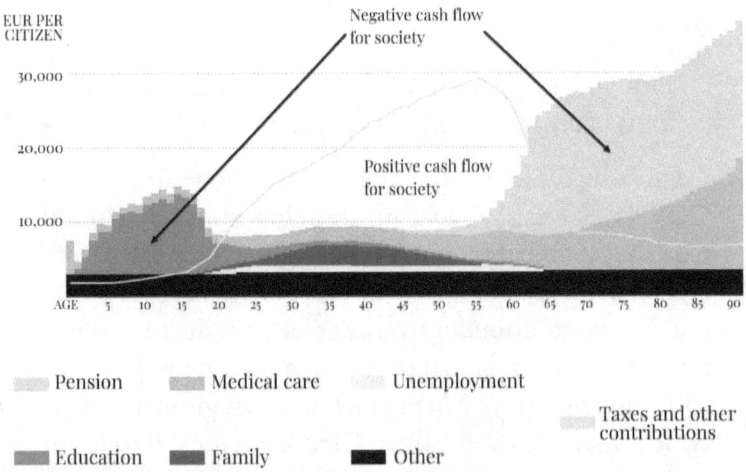

Sources: Bernhard Binder-Hammer. Data: AUSSDA, https://data.aussda.at/dataset.xhtml?persistentId=doi:10.11587/4EOXZ0.
Wittgenstein Centre, https://www.wittgensteincentre.org/en/staff/member/hammer.htm.

modules are imported from China, and there is currently no single significant battery manufacturer in Europe, let alone in Germany. The required overcapacity, the global need for energy transition, and the pricing power of a few key suppliers will all likely lead to a substantial rise in prices. Because energy is essential to virtually all products and services, rising energy prices will also exert significant cost and price pressures across the board in the long term.

Structural deficits: In Germany, countless highway bridges are in a dilapidated state, as is the German rail network. Public buildings have a considerable backlog of renovations. Even today, the German healthcare system sends more faxes than any other country in the world, and there is a significant lag in digitization across all areas of public administration. The German Armed Forces, as the war in Ukraine made clear, only have enough ammunition to last a few days. Numerous tanks, helicopters, and other equipment are not operational. Students' performance continues to decline in the PISA rankings. There is a need for major investment across multiple areas of society. It is clearly apparent that these aren't being financed through spending cuts or tax increases, but through new debt. Even if this debt is labeled as *special funds*, as recently occurred with the €100 billion earmarked for the German military, it still remains debt—and that debt expands the money supply, in turn fueling inflation.

In 2023 and 2024, we observed demands for substantial wage increases from unions and a rise in strikes worldwide. Workers are rightfully demanding compensation for the erosion of their purchasing power. At the same time, most companies cannot bear the resulting cost increases. When extensive strikes occur, as in the 1970s and 1980s, supply decreases. Production slows, and products become scarcer and, therefore, more expensive. Labor costs increase.

Several forces can counteract this trend. One of them is innovation. Through ever-accelerating technological progress, productivity increases, and more goods and services can be produced. For example, the capabilities currently demonstrated by ChatGPT are not only impressive but also clearly show in which areas AI can replace humans, such as call center agents. Unlike in previous decades, this doesn't create unemployment. Instead, it fills positions that otherwise could not be filled. Prosperity rises. Technological progress and higher productivity lead to a greater supply of goods. If the money supply remains constant, prices should actually fall. But inflation overshadows the gains from rising productivity. Put differently, we don't just lose purchasing power from rising prices; we also lose what higher productivity should have given us. The damage inflicted by inflation is greater than just a rise in prices.

The very high inflation of the 1970s was brought under control by significant increases in interest rates. At their peak, U.S. interest rates rose to nearly 20% per year. This path cannot be followed nowadays. A hike of that scale would force governments, companies, and private individuals alike into insolvency.

The great danger of a little inflation is that it can set into motion a self-reinforcing cycle that leads to more and ever-accelerating inflation, which continues until the money itself is completely devalued. A one-time increase in certain prices is not problematic when it is not followed by further price increases. An example of this is a potential rise in food prices following a single adverse harvest. If the next harvest is good, prices will decline. There is no inflation.

However, if price increases lead to further, even stronger price increases, it sets off a self-reinforcing cycle. Low inflation can turn into high inflation and, eventually, hyperinflation.

When inflation leads to more money printing, it lays the groundwork for yet more inflation. In the wake of the war in Ukraine and the resulting increase in energy costs, governments responded by implementing debt-financed programs that disbursed funds directly to citizens on a large scale. We saw something similar happen during the COVID-19 crisis, where grants and super-low-interest loans pumped in huge amounts of new money to save the economy. This led to a substantial rise in inflation even before the war in Ukraine had begun. When rising prices in this environment trigger further price hikes, for example, through a wage-price spiral, price increases can become self-perpetuating.

The path to hyperinflation occurs when a government is forced to finance its expenditure through central bank credit (i.e., by printing money) to maintain public order. The book *When Money Dies: The Nightmare of Deficit Spending, Devaluation, and Hyperinflation in Weimar Germany* describes this process during the 1923 Weimar hyperinflation.[4]

When confidence in the intrinsic value of a currency is lost, access to capital markets dries up, and foreign creditors in particular begin demanding more and more of it in exchange for their goods and services—that is, as the external value of the currency continues to fall—this leads to a boom in exports and rising profits for export-oriented companies as well as an ever-increasing money supply. Daniel Stelter describes this process vividly in an episode from his podcast on February 5, 2023.[5]

Even without the very rapid devaluation of money seen in hyperinflation, money still loses almost all its value in the very long term. Over the course of a century, every currency has depreciated by at least 90%. This is shown in the following figure, which illustrates the value of the U.S. dollar relative to officially measured inflation (compared with consumer goods, i.e., measured against the U.S. consumer basket) and to other scarce assets (gold, stocks, and real estate in Miami).

FIGURE 3 (p. 23): Loss of value of the U.S. dollar relative to official inflation and other assets over one hundred years

Why would deflation be so bad?

In the 19th century, during the era of the gold standard, inflationary and deflationary phases alternated. Both phases were short. Booms and busts, upturns, and recessions occurred more frequently but were less extreme. Downturns corrected the excesses and misallocations of the boom years. Companies that weren't profitable in the long

USD vs. Various Assets, 1923–2023

The dollar has lost an average of 7% annually relative to scarce, desirable assets over the past century

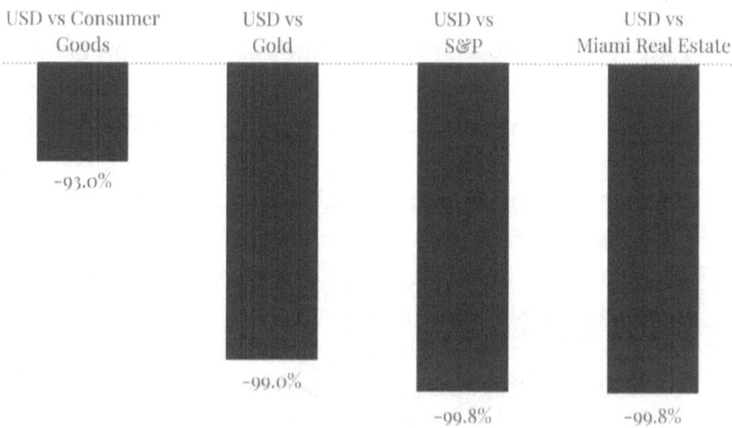

Source: Strategy[8] (formerly MicroStrategy)

term failed, and there was a clear incentive for the surviving ones to operate profitably. Valuable resources were freed up. The government intervened only in the worst cases of hardship and emergency.

The more inflated a system becomes, the more pronounced its adjustment processes are. The greater the excesses and misallocations, the more painful the correction. This means that, in today's system, unlike during the 19th-century gold standard, deflation would be a problem. The adjustment processes would be massive. Companies would fail en masse, unemployment would skyrocket worldwide, tax revenues would plummet, while at the same time government spending would explode. With debt levels so high, borrowers would be crushed by high interest payments, and losses would quickly wipe out equity. In a debt-driven system, insolvency occurs much more quickly. Sustained deflation would push the entire financial system to the brink of collapse or even cause it to collapse.

In other words, deflation in a highly indebted system would be very bad. The Great Depression of 1929 would look like an appetizer by comparison. This means that, regardless of the cost, the system must be protected from deflationary shocks. It must continue to inflate. We observed this in late 2022 and early 2023—even during its interest rate-hike cycle, the ECB continued to buy Italian government bonds to limit the rise in interest rates on these securities. The Bank of Japan did the same. In early 2023, they bought Japanese government bonds on a massive scale to cap the rise in interest rates. The Bank of England did the same; in

March 2023, it stepped in to buy huge amounts of ten-year British government bonds to prevent pension funds from becoming illiquid. In the same month, numerous banks collapsed in the U.S. Even amid high global inflation and, in some cases, shrinking central bank balance sheets, fiscal policy has remained at least partially expansionary through rising debt. Estimates place the U.S. budget deficit for 2024 at $1.8 trillion—approximately 6.4% of gross domestic product—with interest payments alone projected at $1.2 trillion out of government revenue of roughly $5 trillion.[6]

A clear conclusion follows. It is increasingly unlikely that actual inflation will sustainably return to the original 2% target. Unlike in the 1970s, central banks no longer have the ability to raise interest rates sufficiently to curb inflation effectively and permanently. Higher interest rates now only accelerate the debt spiral, as we see in the U.S. in 2025. Additionally, the deflationary forces that once kept prices down—such as globalization and the entry of baby boomers into the workforce—are now, at the time of writing, beginning to reverse.

Despite all of this, in Germany we can be grateful for the democratic order and economic system that have brought us such remarkable prosperity, especially by international standards. But inflation and the significant devaluation of our money are, unfortunately, an inherent part of this system. The upside is that it avoids deflationary shocks. The downsides are numerous. Only very few manage—either through sheer hard work or making sound investment decisions—to escape inflation economically.

What does this have to do with Bitcoin?

Accessible to all, Bitcoin offers a way out of an increasingly inflationary system.

Bitcoin is capped at 21 million units. Slowly but surely, that limit will be reached around the year 2140. Nearly 20 million bitcoin already exist. In ten years, by 2035, 99% of all bitcoin will have been mined, and over approximately the following one hundred years, the total supply of bitcoin will only expand by another 1%. The maximum amount of 21 million cannot be exceeded. We know precisely both the expected annual increase of bitcoin and the maximum supply.

What makes Bitcoin distinctive is that no one can change these fundamental principles. The software is open source and can, in principle, be copied or changed at any time; which sounds like a contradiction but isn't. Numerous copies of the Bitcoin software have already been made, but they've completely withered away. What's crucial to the acceptance of a Bitcoin copy is its user network. Without users, there is no relevance. Bitcoiners want Bitcoin to remain largely as it is; accordingly, it does. If changes occur that do not serve the broader community, they simply don't catch on. No one wants to devalue their own money by increasing the total bitcoin supply.

Chapter 2:
Circa 1943—During World War II

In the home of an elderly retired officer, everything was scarce. Times were difficult and marked by hardship.

One of my grandmother's most carefully guarded treasures was a bottle of schnapps. She kept it tucked away for even darker days, or maybe for the future good ones.

My grandfather reached the point where he was fed up with these dark times and wanted to drink schnapps. But he wasn't allowed to. My grandmother threatened him and forbade him from touching the bottle. She was a force to be reckoned with.

My grandfather didn't like that one bit. Dissatisfied and grumpy, he had been worn down by hard times, his marriage, and the loss of two of his sons. He opened the bottle, took a sip, and put it back. Immediately, he was overcome with guilt and fear of my grandmother.

Clever as he was, he came up with an idea. He simply topped up the missing sip with a little water. The schnapps

bottle looked untouched. No one noticed a thing. And anyway, one time didn't really count. But eventually, he helped himself to another sip and topped up the bottle with water again. Then again. And again.

Of course, the inevitable happened. One fine day, my grandmother opened the bottle only to discover that the schnapps had been thoroughly watered down and was now practically undrinkable. The ensuing fight was explosive, and domestic peace was seriously disrupted. The diluted schnapps was poured down the drain.

What does this have to do with Bitcoin?

Bitcoin is the first, and possibly only, money that cannot be diluted. As it is hard coded into the software, new transactions are bundled into a block and added to the blockchain roughly every ten minutes on average, or as we Bitcoiners say, a block is *mined*. The miners—the ones who write the block, that is, the dataset, into the database—receive a reward for this, known as the *block reward*. That reward is currently 3.125 bitcoin per block, plus the transaction fees associated with all transactions in that block. Every 210,000 blocks (approximately every four years), the reward for miners is halved; this occurred most recently in April 2024. This regular halving of newly created bitcoin via block rewards gradually slows the increase in the total supply of bitcoin as it approaches the cap of 21 million. This cap will be reached around the year 2140. Today, the annual growth rate of the bitcoin supply is less than 1%. It is impossible, however, to create more bitcoin beyond the maximum supply. The existing supply cannot be diluted by the planned issuance.

It's a very different story with sovereign currencies—also known as fiat currencies—such as the dollar, euro, pound, or Swiss franc. The increase or dilution of such currencies is unpredictable, and in some cases, uncontrollable. For decades, they've been diluted at an average annual rate of about 4–8%, and at times over 20%, as measured by the growth of the money supply. Our fiat money essentially consists of debt. Only a small portion is represented by coins and banknotes. When new debt is created, so is new money.[7]

Those who receive the newly created money get to enjoy *the first sip from the bottle*, just like my grandfather. For everyone else, the money loses value. Newly created money devalues and waters down the value of existing money until it eventually becomes unusable, in other words, worthless. We're currently seeing this happen in Turkey, Argentina, and Zimbabwe, among many other countries. In Germany, we've seen it twice in the last hundred years—during the hyperinflation of 1923 after World War I and again right after World War II. Even the ancient Romans secretly reduced the gold content of the coins they issued, effectively diluting the currency. The consequences were devastating. The peace of the Western Roman Empire was seriously disturbed, and as a result, the entire empire collapsed in AD 476.

A little bit of dilution goes unnoticed at first. That's why my grandfather kept going until eventually the schnapps became *undrinkable.* A little bit of currency dilution isn't noticeable either. But over many years, watered-down currencies become increasingly undrinkable. They buy you less and less, and eventually maybe buy you nothing at all.

Bitcoin, however, cannot be diluted beyond 21 million.

Chapter 3:
The Hyperinflation of 1971 at the Kindergarten

I'm pretty sure it was 1971, but it could have been 1972. In any case, it was in kindergarten, and I was five years old. Our teachers had set up a system to motivate us kids to behave well. They had hung a big board on the wall, with all of our names listed. If you were particularly well-behaved, kind, helpful, or polite, they drew a black dot next to your name. Misbehave, and they gave you a red one. It was all about following the kindergarten rules, and the absolute transparency of it motivated most of us to try our best.

At some point, an extra prize was introduced for exceptionally good behavior: a small piece of fabric. From the group's standpoint, that was worth much more than the top ranking in a row of black dots. And it was tangible. You could prove your elite status, even out in the sandbox.

Eventually, a trading system developed between us kids. For a scrap of fabric, you could get a bucket of sifted sand. For two, you could get a piece of candy. Suddenly, we could trade labor (sifting sand) for status symbols or sweets.

Then one day, a new teacher arrived. For whatever reason, she much more generously handed out those scraps of fabric. She simply changed the rules governing their distribution. All of a sudden, everyone had them, and you had to spend four for a piece of candy instead of two. Some of the kids started to complain. Their hard-earned scraps of fabric were now worth less, and they demanded more of them.

As you'd expect, the fabric scraps were given out more and more freely. Before long, anyone could take as many as they wanted. Eventually, they were lying around all over the place. They were worthless. No one wanted them anymore. You couldn't trade them for anything. And so, at just five years old, I experienced genuine hyperinflation.

What does this have to do with Bitcoin?

In kindergarten, the rules were simply changed. The new teacher wanted to be nice, we kids whined, and suddenly more and more fabric scraps were handed out.

The rules of Bitcoin simply cannot be changed.

It's a completely different story with our fiat currencies. They too have rules. The problem is that no one can ensure those rules are actually followed. Here is an example: the European Central Bank is not allowed to permanently finance governments through bond purchases, yet it does so anyway, brazenly and with no one doing—or even being able to do—anything about it. And who would intervene anyway?

Here's another example. The Maastricht Treaty's Stability and Growth Pact stipulated that the budget deficits of EU member states could not exceed 3% of their GDP, although permissible exceptions were built in. However, between 2000 and 2010, the Stability Criteria were repeatedly violated without sanctions—not only by Greece (11 times) but also by larger countries such as Italy (seven times), France (six times), and Germany (five times). According to the Maastricht Treaty, there are clear sanctions for countries that unlawfully fail to adhere to the deficit limit. But not once has such a sanction been imposed. No attempt was ever even made.[8]

This may have been politically expedient and justified for whatever reason, but it shows how difficult it is for us to adhere to the rules. It's like the New Year's resolutions that we make with the greatest of convictions, but then usually don't stick to for very long.

The result is what matters. Currencies inflate and, sooner or later, become worthless. The U.S. dollar has lost 97% of its value over the last hundred years. The British pound, which originally represented a pound of silver, has suffered the same fate. All because more and more new dollars, euros, or pounds have been created, or to put it differently, printed.

The outcome is the same: when the fabric scraps become worthless, everyone who holds them loses their wealth.

This cannot happen with Bitcoin. Its rules are fixed, and no one controls the system nor can they simply change those rules.

Chapter 4:
Easter Bunnies That Were Never Eaten

When I was a little boy, we were given Santa-shaped chocolates for Christmas and chocolate bunnies for Easter.

But I never ate them.

Instead, I lined them up on top of my wardrobe. I liked looking at them. In a way, they were my treasure. I was the only one in the family who had any left. I'd save them for later, thinking I might need them one day.

One or two fell from the wardrobe and broke, and eventually they were discarded. They'd probably become inedible anyway, and by then I'd lost interest in them.

What does this have to do with Bitcoin?

Two things follow. We must practice restraint today if we want to have more tomorrow. But, it is very difficult to carry the value of that restraint into the future. Chocolate spoils eventually and, sooner or later, will become worthless.

Take the fisherman who trades part of his catch to buy materials for a big fishing net. He is sacrificing short-term consumption. He then works additional hours making the net, sacrificing his free time. The next day, instead of going fishing, he forgoes the chance of another catch to work on his net again. By our standards, he is worse off in the short term because he consumes less and works more.

But the next time he goes out to sea—with his net instead of a fishing rod—he catches many more fish. He is now much better off. He can eat more, sell the surplus fish, or trade them to hire workers to build a larger boat. He could extend his house or pay for his children's education. Because he showed restraint today, he and others are better off tomorrow.

If the fisherman builds a bad net that tears and becomes useless the first time he tries it out, he's simply had a bit of bad luck. He is a little worse off, and his sacrifices haven't paid off this time. He has given up his own consumption and spare time and gotten nothing in return. Now, if he's smart, he will learn from his mistake and build or acquire a better net the second time around.

The fisherman's short-term *crisis* of saving and sacrificing consumption is something we barely tolerate nowadays. Even renowned economists describe saving as harmful to the economy. They claim it drains demand and shrinks the economy. Instead, they argue it is better to stimulate consumption by any means possible. This happens through government spending programs and debt, which ultimately lead to inflation. And price rises encourage more unsustainable, needless consumption. We purchase inexpensive toys, food, and clothing because we can no longer afford higher prices. They are *cheap* only relative to the new, inflated prices. We buy things today that we don't really need because tomorrow everything is going to be more expensive, and we won't be able to afford them anymore.

This is not good. Above all, it's harmful to the environment, which is being overexploited. It's bad because we fail to save, meaning we don't build up the capital that could drive greater productivity and thus a higher standard of living in the future. It's bad because we can no longer tolerate even the smallest sacrifices, because we think more and more in the short term and make far fewer decisions that pay off in the long run. Our time preference increases, which means we want everything as soon as possible. To sustain short-term demand, society is conditioned to consume, think, and act in the short term, regardless of the cost. And it makes sense. If my money is worth less in the future, I might as well buy the things today that I may only need tomorrow.

The fisherman can't save for very long. His fish remains edible for only a few days at most. After that, he has to head back out to sea and catch more.

Unlike with fiat money, where literally any amount of new currency can be created, there will never be more than 21 million bitcoin in existence. Beyond that, no more bitcoin will ever be in circulation.

And unlike chocolate bunnies or freshly caught fish, bitcoin doesn't spoil. It lasts forever, can be taken anywhere because it's digital, and can easily be stored at minimal cost. But be careful with your financial planning. In the short term—even over two or three years—the value of bitcoin can fluctuate wildly when measured in traditional currencies. For this reason, it makes sense to extend your savings horizon for bitcoin to at least four or five years.

The value of a network grows disproportionately with the number of users in that network. With growing adoption and usage, the value of bitcoin actually rises because more people are actively using it, or building new networks on top of it, which overall boosts demand for this increasingly scarce good. Since 2009, there has never been a five-year period in which bitcoin has lost value. Of course, that's no guarantee. Still, it is a solid rule of thumb when deciding on the minimum investment time one should consider as a bitcoin saver.

Bitcoin encourages individuals not to spend their hard-earned assets immediately, but to save them for later. Looking beyond the short-term makes long-term thinking, planning, and investing possible. Bitcoin motivates us to reduce short-term consumption and invest for the future—an investment that, if well thought out and successful, should improve productivity and thus prosperity, instead of us simply burning through our resources in the short term. Once you realize that an increasing number of people are recognizing these advantages and choosing to store part of their savings in bitcoin, the trend becomes clear. Bitcoin remains an attractive store of value today, tomorrow, and well into the future. So, bitcoin is both a strong store of value and an excellent long-term investment.

Chapter 5:
The Work-Time Savings Account

As a little boy, I always wished I could have a time savings account. Sometimes, when I was bored, I would have liked to deposit that time into a savings account and then withdraw it later—like when I left for the bus too late and it drove off right in front of me, or when Christmas was coming and I still hadn't finished making all the gifts. That way, I could withdraw a few minutes from my time savings account and catch the bus I missed.

I thought about this a lot. That idea sparked a fascination with science fiction, time travel, and personal planning—and, more broadly, with innovation. Innovations often save time, after all. For instance, shopping online saves a trip into town, the time spent searching for a parking spot, and the walk through a store. If we manage ourselves well, we can often tackle tasks ahead of time that we'd normally have to do later on. That way, the time we invest today becomes available to us in the future.

ZEIT
SPAR
BUCH

What does this have to do with Bitcoin?

Bitcoin is a time-saving account. Through bitcoin, we can transfer time from today to tomorrow, and to the day after. The lifetime we spend working to earn money can be stored in bitcoin and retrieved later. Unlike saving it in euros or dollars, its value remains stable and can even increase over the long term.

As we saw in my example of the newspaper boy and a scoop of ice cream, the German mark and the euro are not suitable for storing work and lifetime value in the long run. Measured in scoops of ice cream (and many other goods), only a very small portion of that time could be carried into the future. Over roughly forty years, 80–90% of the value of one's work time, as measured in scoops of ice cream, has been lost.

I first wrote this passage in August 2023. At the time, the value of bitcoin was approximately €27,000, nearly equal to the median net salary in Germany, which was approximately €26,000. This meant that at that point in time, you could store the value of one year's work in the form of one bitcoin. When I revised this passage at the end of September 2024, the value of bitcoin had risen to €57,000. That year of work time had now more than doubled. By January 2026, with the value of bitcoin at approximately €85,000, the same work from August 2023 had more than tripled.

In the short term, it appears that bitcoin can not only transfer a year's worth of work into the future but also yield good returns, a bit like a savings account. In 2023, the official inflation rate, according to the Federal Statistical

Office, was 5.9%. Based on a net salary of €26,000, this corresponded to a loss of €1,456 in purchasing power. Put in the context of workdays, of which there are two hundred fifty per year (excluding vacations), that's the equivalent of fourteen workdays—almost three weeks. Three weeks of our working lives were lost to inflation in one year. Bitcoin, by contrast, was able to easily carry the value of a year's work into the future. Additionally, it yielded a 100% return. A year of work was valued at two years, and by January 2025, it was valued at almost four years of work.

While we won't speculate at this point about the possible development of bitcoin's value, it seems inevitable that if bitcoin continues to gain traction over the long term, the price will continue to rise—though likely at a continuously decreasing rate of growth. If bitcoin were to assume a role similar to gold as a store of value and reached the value of all gold, about $28.5 trillion, that would correspond to a bitcoin value of nearly $1.3 million as of late 2025. This could either happen decades from now or possibly even as early as the 2030s. It means that a net annual salary from August 2023 could (optimistically speaking) become the equivalent of a good 30–50 net annual salaries for the average German in about ten years. By contrast, if you were to put your net annual salary in an interest-free checking account over a decade with inflation running at 4%, you'd lose about a third of its purchasing power. For twelve months of work, you would end up with the equivalent of only eight months. In that same scenario, holding just 1 bitcoin could transfer so much value into the future that it would fund an entire retirement, based on an average retirement period of twenty years (mean for men and women).[9]

Any 22-year-old who graduates with a bachelor's degree today is likely to face approximately fifty years of work before retirement. Over the same period of time, if bitcoin continues to gain traction, it is quite possible that the fraction of a bitcoin that is equal to today's net annual salary might end up being worth the equivalent of 30 or maybe many more annual salaries. This means that with just a fraction of one bitcoin, not only can you transport the value of today's work into the future, but you can also earn an attractive return on the time you deposited.

Many years' worth of work could be transported into the future at a good rate of interest. Instead of retiring at age seventy, the graduates who manage to store their net annual salary in bitcoin today might be able to retire at fifty, forty, or even earlier. Perhaps they could use it to buy a home or to pay for their children's expensive education. Or to build a productive company—all because they could afford to take the risk.

One sensible bitcoin allocation strategy for someone just starting their career, for instance, might be to store the equivalent of one net annual salary in bitcoin. As of October 2025, that would be about 0.3 bitcoin.

Bitcoin is the time savings account that I'd always wished for as a child.

Section 2: Bitcoin—Protection Against an Increasingly Unstable Financial System

LB
$

Chapter 6:

2007–2009—The Global Financial Crisis and the Birth of Bitcoin

As a supplement to reading this chapter, you can also read Michael Lewis's book The Big Short *(later made into a movie). It illustrates the collapse of the financial system during the 2008 mortgage crisis and the response of governments and central banks, printing money.*

On January 1, 2000, the world was supposed to end. As the date changed and the next millennium rolled in, computer systems programmed in the 1960s and 1970s were to crash. Storage space was very expensive back then. As a result, programmers often saved space by recording years with only two digits instead of four, omitting the century. Once the century changed, the logic would be lost, and systems would malfunction.

Massive IT projects were launched to fix the problem and prevent looming disasters, like nuclear power plants exploding. Alongside a booming tech industry, an even more booming survival industry emerged. Guidebooks were published on how to survive the impending catastrophe (*hide under the table*), while there was a healthy trade in bunkers and overpriced survival packs.

In a preemptive move, the U.S. Federal Reserve loosened monetary policy. The burgeoning internet and its early successes that had brought technology to the masses. Together with the loose financing conditions and growing public enthusiasm at the turn of the millennium this ignited a unique boom on the stock markets, especially for tech and internet stocks.

The world did not come to an end. Instead, people started to wonder what would become of companies that had no chance of turning a profit and depended on continuous injections of investor funding. Doubts began to spread, share prices started to fall, and over the course of the year 2000, the dot-com bubble burst.

The final nail in the coffin of the 2000s bubble came on September 11, 2001. The terrorist attack on the World Trade Center in New York made it seem as though the world really was ending. Air traffic shut down, war broke out, and a recession followed. Stock markets plunged, and they just kept falling.

Once again, the U.S. Federal Reserve stepped in to save the economy and the financial markets. Interest rates were slashed, credit became cheap, and with this, the economic downturn was slowed. Starting in early 2003, the stock markets began to recover. Slowly at first, then faster. The exceptionally low interest rates stimulated economic activity, albeit not as intended. The burst tech bubble was soon replaced by a gigantic housing bubble, especially in the United States.

The film *The Big Short* begins with a quote from Mark Twain:

> *It ain't what you don't know that gets you into trouble. It's what you know for sure that just ain't so.*

History provides us with many examples that show how stubbornly and for how long people, indeed entire societies, have clung to false beliefs. A good example is the geocentric worldview that many held in the Middle Ages: they believed that the universe revolved around the Earth. Galileo Galilei held an opposing belief and was threatened with death and excommunicated from the Church for it. The Church's self-image and vested interests forbade such an inconvenient truth. But as it is with the truth, a point comes when it can no longer be denied.

The same was true of the financial crisis of 2007–2009. Behind many financial products on offer were mortgage-backed securities of little or no value. This truth, too, eventually could not be denied. The markets for these securities and the financial products built on them collapsed, along with a lot of the banks and financial institutions that held them. In the end, the entire financial system imploded. Major, well-known banks went bankrupt, financial markets dried up, and even healthy companies were put at risk of failure.

The terrifying yet fascinating part was the reaction of governments and central banks—through bailouts. With the exception of Lehman Brothers and a few others, virtually all the major institutions were saved. At the time, Chancellor Angela Merkel guaranteed the German public that their bank deposits were safe—a promise she likely could not have kept if it had been called out. The central element of the bailouts was and still is the printing of money. Governments generously rescued important, systemically relevant banks and companies with the input of fresh money. Central banks financed and continue to finance this by purchasing government bonds, cutting interest rates, and providing very favorable financing conditions to banks.

This point is very important. When a central bank buys an outstanding government bond, that means it is increasing the money supply or *printing money*. In the film Oeconomia, Peter Praet, at that time the chief economist of the ECB, says this quite explicitly,[10] "It is not physical money, but electronic." Printing money means increasing the amount of money in circulation. And that results in all of our money getting *watered down*. Ultimately, this makes it worth less since there's more money but the same amount of goods.

When new money is created—that is, when money is inflated and then spent, no matter what it's spent on—prices will eventually rise, and the money everyone else holds becomes less valuable. Put another way, when new money is created, everyone who already holds money is slightly dispossessed. Only those who receive the new money first benefit, which is usually the banks, shareholders, and companies as well as borrowers and thus the government. Also benefiting are those who hold the goods or assets that are first purchased with the newly created money. This primarily includes real estate, stocks, and tangible assets in general.

Such inflation must be distinguished from individual price increases. If the demand for city-center locations suddenly rises because people are moving from the country to the city, property prices in city centers will rise, while they fall in the countryside. With inflation, prices rise almost everywhere. Price increases caused by rising demand or falling supply, such as after a poor harvest, are limited and are offset by a drop in prices elsewhere.

Inflation acts like a tax, but it isn't perceived as such. The government could just as well take a small amount of money from every business and citizen to cover its spending instead of creating new money by issuing a government bond. In practice, it would be the same thing, only it wouldn't be so easy, and many people would complain and might vote those politicians out in the next election. Inflation is vague, and in public perception it's not the government's fault but rather that of others who are creating shortages of goods and profiting from rising prices. Political and public scapegoats for rising prices can always be found.

The former ECB chief economist, Peter Praet, states quite clearly that the functioning of today's financial and economic system depends on the creation of more and more money—in other words, on continuous inflation. If the last financial crises have shown us anything, it's the automatic reaction of governments—printing money. And crises will always keep coming for a variety of reasons: the ongoing climate crisis, pandemics, wars, migration, demographics, etc. Justification and excuses for printing money can always be found.

What does this have to do with Bitcoin?

A major and very valid criticism of a sound monetary system, in which money cannot be multiplied uncontrollably, is that it provides no way to intervene quickly by increasing the money supply in severe crises. That's true. You would have to save beforehand, to set aside reserves. And if there is one thing politicians cannot do, it's save. There is always a good reason to spend money, whether it's simply doing good, solving problems, winning over voters before an election, or even supporting a friendly entrepreneur in one's own constituency. The alternative would be to raise taxes in order to finance these unforeseen expenses. That would be politically and economically counterproductive. It would scare off voters and take away their purchasing power.

The crucial point is this: without the ability to print money at will, the boom that precedes a crisis wouldn't arise in the first place, or at the very least would be much smaller. And the subsequent crises would also be a lot smaller. This is evident in the economic cycles of the 19th century, when a strict gold standard was in place. Yes, there were numerous crises at the time. But they were short and less severe. And periods of falling prices certainly did not end in the dreaded deflationary spiral.

The ability to print unlimited amounts of money leads to correspondingly large misallocations, which then lead to correspondingly large corrections, and therefore, crises. These crises in turn trigger even more money-printing, and on it goes.

The greater the misallocations beforehand, the greater the corrections afterward. A healthy monetary system leads to sounder economic decisions, sustainable upturns, and brief downturns in which misallocations are corrected. Money that cannot be arbitrarily multiplied limits misallocations during a boom, and accordingly, limits corrections during a downturn.

At the height of the financial crisis, on October 31, 2008, an anonymous person or group published the Bitcoin white paper—six weeks after Lehman Brothers, one of the largest banks in the U.S., filed for bankruptcy. On January 3, 2009, Satoshi Nakamoto launched the Bitcoin blockchain. The very first block was mined. This first block contains the following message:

> *The Times 03/Jan/2009 Chancellor on brink of second bailout for banks*

This was an explicit reference to a headline in The Times on January 3, 2009—the repeated bailout of a financial system still teetering on the brink of collapse.

Bitcoin was, and still is, the answer to a fragile financial system: to uncontrolled money printing, to willful denial of reality, but also to the unfair and socially unjust expropriation that accompanies money creation.

The cap of 21 million bitcoin and the lack of central control make a policy of inflation impossible. Someone who holds bitcoin cannot be dispossessed by the uncontrolled printing of even more bitcoin. Nor can they be dispossessed by banks that go bankrupt or deny access to bitcoin, provided they hold their bitcoin in a self-hosted wallet and thereby manage their own access. No central authority can revoke that access.

The timing of Bitcoin's launch was no coincidence. It was the reaction to a financial system that would have collapsed had money not been printed in a pretty much uncontrolled manner. Bitcoin is sound money—a response to a broken financial system. It is a system that is not imposed from above. Participation is voluntary and open to anyone. No one with a computer or smartphone and an internet connection can be excluded from it. For many, it's a lifeline out of the fiat money system that is not sustainably viable. In contrast to an inflationary and opaque system, Bitcoin is decentralized, transparent, and fundamentally honest.

Chapter 7: Breaking Free from a Crisis-Ridden Financial System

Toward the end of World War II, my grandfather fled with his family from Königsberg in what was then East Prussia to West Germany. He was a seed merchant. He sent three sacks of seeds ahead of him. Two ended up in East Germany and were lost. One arrived in the West and became the foundation for his new, successful life.

I heard this story repeatedly as a young boy and learned the lesson. Diversify and exit a failing system.

In 2016, Deutsche Bank's stock accelerated the decline that had begun in 2008. From late summer 2015 to spring 2016, its share price almost halved, falling from €28.50 on July 31, 2015, to €15.30 on April 28, 2016. Zerohedge.com reported on this regularly. The broader context was alarming. One of the world's largest banks, with a derivatives portfolio of around €50 trillion—more than 10 times Germany's GNP—and just €60 billion in actual equity, not to mention *data integrity issues* in its IT systems, was

on the verge of failure. The capital markets seemed to be losing confidence in Deutsche Bank. ZeroHedge went a step further and compared the performance of Deutsche Bank's stock to that of Lehman Brothers. The parallels were frightening.

In the 2007–2009 financial crisis, we had already seen what happens when confidence in a bank is lost: it fails. Without confidence, a bank loses access to the necessary sources of funding, and once cut off from them, it becomes insolvent. The same dynamic threatened to play out again in 2011, when the government bonds of southern EU member states suddenly fell sharply, and interest rates skyrocketed accordingly. Suddenly, debt sustainability was called into question. Italy, for example, one of the EU's largest economies, appeared to be on the path to insolvency. Mario Draghi averted disaster with his famous *Whatever it takes* speech, showing that the ECB would do everything necessary to prevent collapse—which ultimately meant buying government bonds (i.e., expanding the money supply) and lowering interest rates to stave off one or more sovereign defaults.

In 2013, an example was made of the small country of Cyprus. Its banks either collapsed or were *rescued* by imposing large losses on deposits exceeding €100,000 through a bail-in. Around this time, bitcoin would rise from about $10 at the start of 2013 to over $1,000 by November of that year.

The facts are plain and simple. Time and again, a crucial part of the financial system teeters on the edge of collapse.

Ultimately, there are only two options: print money or accept a collapse with all its adverse consequences. Ultimately, printing money is the easier and, above all, far more politically acceptable solution.

Over the summer and into the fall of 2016, Deutsche Bank's share price moved in parallel with that of Lehman Brothers in 2008. The comparable point at which Lehman lost all trust and failed, for Deutsche Bank, corresponded to a share price of €10. As soon as the price fell below that, the bank would go bankrupt, according to ZeroHedge. In September 2016, that moment arrived. On September 26, the share price dipped below €10. By September 30, it had dropped below €9.[11]

During that time, I drove to the local Deutsche Bank branch during my lunch break and requested a low five-figure cash withdrawal. They wouldn't give me the money because it wasn't there. I stood at the counter, completely speechless. *Had the bank already collapsed?* Was I too late?

Asking nicely helped, and I was eventually able to get my money. Nevertheless, one thing became perfectly clear: when it really matters, you can't count on being able to access your own money. The money in your bank account is not even really yours. It's a claim against the bank; in other words, you are giving the bank a loan. If the bank cannot honor that loan, you quite simply won't get back the money that you're owed. Incidentally, the fact that the bank owes you money is also the reason you get interest at all when you *put your money in the bank.*

That was the moment it became clear to me. If it were possible for the financial system to collapse, I would have to withdraw at least part of my money from that system well in advance. Because inside the system, at the very least it was at risk, maybe even partially lost. Ultimately, there are only a few concrete ways to achieve this, including having physical gold in your own possession, and holding bitcoin. Other assets, such as antiques and Rolex watches, may also lie outside the system, but they're often unwieldy and less liquid. A Rolex can also be a well-made counterfeit, and the antiques market has collapsed in recent years. Antiques no longer suit the tastes of the younger generation.

Bitcoin, by contrast, has three decisive advantages over gold:

- Bitcoin is extremely easy to transport.
- The private key—the access key to the bitcoin you own that is stored on the blockchain—can be written down on a slip of paper or, if need be, even memorized.
- And bitcoin's authenticity can easily be verified on the blockchain.

Transport and authentication aren't so easy with gold. Transporting it can be cumbersome, and throughout history, governments have repeatedly confiscated gold. In addition, it is neither fast nor easy to verify that a bar is solid gold rather than a tungsten core plated in gold. Gold is physical; bitcoin is digital. And bitcoin can easily be divided into any amount, making it suitable for even the smallest transactions.

Cash has a value, meanwhile, that's still part of the system. With the growing push toward a cashless society, cash is now primarily suitable for small transactions. India's sudden demonetization of the ₹100 note in November 2016 demonstrated how quickly cash can be devalued and revealed for what it essentially is: printed paper.

Nevertheless, in September 2016, I put a little *printed paper* in the safe, picked up some gold, and—though my trust in Bitcoin was significantly lower back then—bought a small amount of bitcoin. In retrospect, the latter turned out to be the best decision by far, even though Deutsche Bank did, fortunately, recover, and neither people's deposits nor the wider financial system came under direct threat.

A few years later, I learned from someone close to the Deutsche Bank board that the bank was at acute risk of default by the end of September 2016. Speculative attacks by hedge funds against Deutsche Bank had reportedly been fended off through intergovernmental communication.

Section 3:
The Adoption of Bitcoin

Chapter 8: Love at Second or Third Sight, and the Spark in Jan and Jörg's Eyes

I first met Jörg von Minckwitz in 2013 at an event hosted by the then–Economics Minister Philipp Rösler, who had invited Peter Thiel as a guest. At the time, Jörg and his co-founder, Jan Goslicki, were planning to launch various Bitcoin startups. There was a spark in his eyes as he told me about all kinds of business ideas. I didn't understand them, and it didn't click for me. It wasn't until two years later, at the end of 2015, that I would take a closer look at Bitcoin.

Peter Thiel shared his formula for truly great investments that day. Look for big ideas that no one else has recognized yet. He asked, "What important truth do very few people agree with you on?" Nothing came to mind in that moment. All the major ideas that occurred to me weren't new and had already been widely discussed.

I left the event with it still gnawing at me that I couldn't come up with a big, as-yet-undiscovered idea. The only thing that came to mind was that the financial system itself was in the process of falling apart. In Cyprus, large deposits had just been seized to save the banks—the first major European bail-in. The Greek debt crisis had only passed two years earlier, and then–ECB President Mario Draghi had barely managed to contain the sharp rise in Italian government bond yields with his now famous *whatever it takes* statement. Yes, the state of the financial system was certainly a big problem—a major one—and it was largely overlooked.

But startups in that space? It just didn't click.

I kept hearing about blockchain, cryptocurrencies, and of course Bitcoin. But in my view at the time, even the limited supply of bitcoin couldn't serve as a hedge against inflation. It seemed to me that even though the number of bitcoin might be capped, the number of cryptocurrencies was unlimited. Bitcoin simply didn't make any sense to me.

Then, in September 2015, at eight o'clock in the morning in a hotel lobby, I ran into Jörg again, along with his co-founder, Jan. They had launched Bitwala, a few months earlier, a startup that has unfortunately since failed and is attempting a relaunch, and were seeking investment for their fledgling company. Beyond the core idea, the founding team is crucial in the early stages. Jan and Jörg expressed enthusiasm as they discussed Bitcoin and the opportunities they saw related to it. They wanted to use the Bitcoin network to transfer money internationally. It was supposed to be fast, inexpensive, and, above all, operate outside the traditional banking and payment system. The financial crisis was still fresh in everyone's mind. Their idea seemed sensible and full of potential: if you wanted to send money to Africa, for example, they would convert euros into bitcoin, transfer them, and then swap them back into the respective local currency. Even accounting for potential price fluctuations and bitcoin transaction fees, such a transfer would be much cheaper and faster than one handled by the traditional banking system. It was a billion-dollar market, given the sheer scale of money transfers worldwide.

The way Jan and Jörg spoke about Bitcoin was fascinating; their enthusiasm was infectious. Their arguments were solid; the startup could actually work. And their enthusiasm for Bitcoin was unmatched; euphoric, even.

An almost certain way to spot outstanding investments is to look for enthusiasm, especially from passionate customers. When people are willing to stand in line outside stores for hours to buy, for instance, the first iPhone, the product is likely unique and extraordinary. Even without a deep understanding of the product, the company, or the market—the long lines outside of Apple Stores in 2007—were a pretty good indicator that buying Apple stock in 2007 had an outstanding risk-to-reward ratio.

If the first customers make better salespeople than a company's best sales team, you can be pretty sure that the product (therefore the company) has the potential to be a huge success. That's because these customers are inadvertently selling the product around the clock—to their colleagues, their friends, and anyone they bump into at a party. When a product like this comes along, it makes investing in it almost a no-brainer.

Think of the buzz of excitement in the early days of the internet, or those first Amazon customers who raved to all their friends about books that arrived the next day—and later on, sometimes even the same day. Or think of the first Tesla drivers who took every opportunity to eulogize about the user-friendliness of the software and the Supercharger network.

Jan and Jörg were just as enthusiastic about Bitcoin.

It was reason enough for me to finally start getting into it, and my first step was to buy a bitcoin on the then leading German exchange Bitcoin.de. The process was clunky, anything but user-friendly, complicated, tedious, and downright annoying. Just as the internet was before the invention of the browser. However, that bitcoin also cost me just over €300.

I'd taken the first step, and it produced an effect similar to buying a share in a company. Suddenly, you become interested in it and begin to gather more information about it. I began to see news and discussions on Bitcoin everywhere—whether I was reading a newsletter, surfing the internet, or simply in conversation with someone. Above all, I noticed how many people like Jan and Jörg were out there—enthusiasts, fanatics, evangelists who couldn't stop themselves from explaining everything about Bitcoin.

So, I listened. Very slowly, piece by piece, it began to make sense.

Chapter 9: The Power of Network Effects, De Facto Standards, and Apple's Near Collapse in the Mid-1990s

I was a huge Apple fan, as early as 1988. The Apple Macintosh represented the promise of a computer that understood people—approachable, friendly, and above all, user-friendly.

Compared to Microsoft Windows, Apple had the better technology—it was sleeker, more intuitive, and offer more advanced features. And yet, by the mid-1990s, Apple was on the verge of failure. The Apple Macintosh had remained too small, confined to a niche. The Windows/Intel/PC ecosystem, by contrast, seemed too powerful. So powerful, in fact, that Microsoft, as a quasi-monopolist of PC operating systems, came under scrutiny by U.S. antitrust authorities. This was in no small part because of its aggressive actions against Netscape. Microsoft bundled Internet Explorer with the Windows operating system at no cost. It

was preinstalled on every PC and set as the default browser. Netscape suffered considerably as a result, to the point that it was on the verge of collapse, and in early 1999, it was sold to AOL. Microsoft was the *evil* company that swallowed or destroyed weaker competitors. And this strategy worked—until U.S. regulators threatened to break up the company or at least impose very harsh penalties.

It was striking that the obviously inferior technology (Windows) was not only more successful than the superior one (Apple) but also managed to push Apple and all others out of the market, becoming the monopolist and establishing the de facto standard.

Why? Did the market fail? Was it simply chaos that could have ended in any outcome? Why did de facto standards emerge in some markets and not in others? What did it depend on? What could one do to make oneself, or one's own technology, the de facto standard?

These were highly fascinating questions, and I addressed them in my doctoral dissertation.[12]

The main drivers of de facto standards are network effects and economies of scale. Economies of scale ensure that, as adoption increases, costs decrease. But this effect is limited. At some point, costs decrease only marginally, or not at all. Network effects, on the other hand, ensure that as adoption increases, so does the technology's usefulness. This increase can be linear or exponential—the more users, the greater the utility which can accelerate adoption further. As long as this benefit continues to grow with the adoption of a technology, alternative technologies stand virtually no chance. Without adoption, new technologies lack utility in networks. Even if they have greater intrinsic value, the overall utility of established technologies—owing to their large user base—often exceeds that of new, potentially superior technologies. So, the new ones disappear, and usually only one (or very few) winners remain. These are what we call *winner-takes-all* markets.

What do these network effects look like? Well, there are direct and indirect ones. A direct network effect occurs when each additional user provides a direct benefit to all other users. Let's consider a communication network, for example. If I'm the first and only person to have a telephone or WhatsApp, it's a worthless situation. I can't do anything with them. If another person has a phone or uses WhatsApp, the utility is severely limited; I can communicate only with that person. The more people who use a communication network, the more valuable it becomes for everyone. In 1980, Robert Metcalfe described this relationship in what became known as Metcalfe's Law. Put simply, it states that the value of a network is proportional to the square of its user base. In other words, the network utility increases exponentially with the adoption of users.

As long as the increase in utility from growing adoption does not diminish at a certain point—that is, diminishing marginal utility does not set in—then a single, dominant de facto standard naturally emerges. When diminishing marginal utility does occur, which is usually the case, several additional standards can emerge, though typically only a few do. A good example is smartphone operating systems.

Here, not one but two standards have emerged: iOS and Android. Virtually every other alternative operating system, such as Windows, Palm, Psion, Symbian, and all proprietary systems from cell phone manufacturers, have either failed or been relegated to very small niche markets.

In addition to direct network effects, there are indirect network effects in which additional users confer an indirect benefit on everyone else. This can occur through complementary products. For example, a PC supplied with an operating system only is practically useless. You need programs that run on it. That's how an indirect network effect works. The more people who buy PCs with a particular operating system, the more worthwhile it becomes for developers to create compatible programs. The availability, in turn, attracts more users. Indirectly, through the sale of compatible programs, additional users increase the overall value of a technology for others.

What is distinctive about technology is that it can exhibit substantial direct and indirect network effects. The more there are, the stronger they become, and the longer they last. If the additional value continues to increase with a growing number of users, it is more likely that de facto standards will emerge.

What does this have to do with Bitcoin?

Bitcoin is a decentralized technology composed of multiple overlapping networks. These include users, miners, developers, applications, and networks that build on Bitcoin, as well as events, local meetups, and related activities. It's clear that network effects also play a key role in Bitcoin. The more diverse and widespread these network effects are, the larger and more valuable bitcoin will become.

First and foremost, Bitcoin is a technology with a very relevant and significant inherent utility, above all as a store of value but also as a means of payment without intermediaries, independent of the established financial system. It is also a network technology with numerous direct and indirect network effects across a range of user groups, including individuals, companies, governments, and central banks. It is quite clear that the more bitcoin is used, the more useful and therefore valuable it becomes. Just as Windows became the dominant standard for PC operating systems—or as Android and iOS set the standard for smartphone operating systems—bitcoin could evolve into the dominant standard for store-of-value applications. And acting as a store of value is just one of many possible use cases. Others include payments, identity solutions built on Bitcoin, or further networks and services layered on top of the Bitcoin network.

This is already the case within the world of cryptocurrencies. While there are more than 20,000 cryptocurrencies, only a very few are suitable as a store of value due to their properties. For the vast majority of them, the supply of coins isn't capped—either from the start, or because the rules can be changed at any time by a central authority. Among truly decentralized cryptocurrencies comparable to Bitcoin and suitable for serving as a store of value, Bitcoin holds a market share of at least 95% and likely closer to 99%

by market capitalization. In the cryptocurrency ecosystem, Bitcoin has already established itself as the dominant standard.

The crucial question now is whether Bitcoin's network effects are strong enough to establish it as the de facto standard for store-of-value applications both within the crypto space and in the traditional financial system. If that happens, bitcoin's current value potential could increase 50-fold, maybe even 100-fold.

The race is ongoing. At the moment, bitcoin only plays a minor role in the international financial system. Its total market capitalization of $2 trillion in January 2025 is just a fraction of the value in the traditional financial system. But the moment the inherent value of traditional fiat money is eroded by inflation, and once Bitcoin's network effects gain momentum, the balance of stored value will begin to shift. Bitcoin can then take over the store-of-value function from other asset classes.

FIGURE 4 (p. 76): Value of bitcoin compared to other traditional asset classes

Even with low inflation, there is no good, simple store of value in the fiat system. Classic fiat currencies certainly don't qualify, because even at so-called *price stability* (i.e., an inflation rate of 2%), the value of money halves within thirty-five years. That's not stability. At a monetary inflation rate of 7%, measured by the growth of the money supply, the value of money would halve in just ten years. Over thirty years, that would include three halvings, to 50%, then

Bitcoin Is Still Tiny Compared with Other Asset Classes

Overview of Major Asset Classes

Total global asset value:
Approximately $1,000T

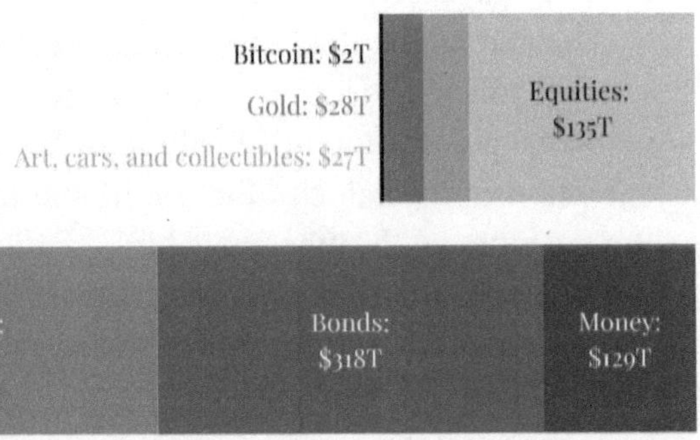

Source: Jesse Myers, onceinaspecies.com

25%, then 12.5%. This means that at 7% annual inflation, 87.5% of the value is lost within thirty years—a near-total loss of purchasing power. If you measure money's loss of value not by the consumer price index but by the expansion of the money supply, the rate in Europe is closer to 5% than 2% when measured by long-term M2 expansion.

With a global money supply of $129 trillion, as shown in the graph above, 5% inflation erodes roughly $6 trillion in purchasing power every year. That's roughly 1.5 times Germany's gross national product.

This ultimately means that cash, as well as money held in checking or savings accounts, is guaranteed to lose purchasing power, and by a significant amount, depending on the inflation rate and the time horizon. This underscores the need to invest funds. That is precisely the point. In the traditional system, preserving the purchasing power of money requires investing it so that the after-tax returns are at least equal to the rate of inflation. Investing involves buying bonds, real estate, stocks, gold, or other assets.

There are two reasons to invest your money: the first is to grow it and try to earn a return. The second is to protect it from inflation devaluation. At first glance, the two motives appear similar, but they are fundamentally different. A bank's financial advisor invests the client's savings and is confident they can grow them. Perhaps they want to build wealth. Meanwhile, a salaried engineer who is nearing retirement—perhaps with a small inheritance—only wants to preserve the value of his money, or more precisely, its purchasing power. He's content with what he has and simply wants to enjoy a worry-free retirement. However, he also invests his money, as it will lose value if he leaves it in the bank. He must invest it, in fact, just to prevent this. Ultimately, capital flows into various asset classes, not only in pursuit of high returns but also, quite simply, to protect against inflation. These asset classes serve as stores of value. In other words, a significant share of the demand for real estate, stocks, or bonds isn't driven by a desire to invest in them per se, but rather by the need to preserve the purchasing power of one's money. Someone might buy a property, for example, just to prevent inflation from eroding the value of their money.

This means that a substantial portion of the total value of stocks, real estate, bonds, and gold derives from the demand for a solid store of value rather than from the pursuit of returns beyond inflation. And we're talking about very large numbers here. The total value of global assets is often estimated at approximately $1,000 trillion. Bitcoin's strong network effects have already made it the de facto standard for storing value among cryptocurrencies. Should these effects extend beyond the crypto space to become the de facto store of value, then bitcoin could absorb portions of the demand currently served by these asset classes. That could raise the current market value of bitcoin—about $2 trillion—into the $100–$200 trillion range. At a maximum supply of 21 million, it's straightforward to calculate the effect this would have on bitcoin's price: around $5–$10 million per bitcoin in today's purchasing-power terms. Add to that the inflation that will have occurred by then, and much higher values are conceivable.

Whether it will come to that is an open question and ultimately remains uncertain. It will depend on how strong Bitcoin's network effects prove to be compared to the diverse and existing network effects of the current financial system. And it will also depend on how the inherent utility of bitcoin as a store of value stacks up against that of the fiat system. As already outlined, there is substantial evidence that inflationary pressures will rise considerably due to deglobalization, demographics, the energy transition, unchecked government activities, massive infrastructure investments, and intensifying global conflicts, with their inevitable accompanying rearmament. All of this provides Bitcoin with a significant tailwind for further adoption and, in turn, for increasing network utility.

Bitcoin's risk/reward profile is highly asymmetric: it has a limited downside balanced against a medium- to long-term upside with a potential upside multiple of 50 to 100. As Satoshi Nakamoto wrote in 2009, "It might make sense to get some in case it catches on. If enough people think the same way, it will become a self-fulfilling prophecy."[13]

Hal Finney, one of Satoshi Nakamoto's closest contacts, wrote in early 2011 when the bitcoin price was still below one U.S. dollar:

> *Since we're all rich with Bitcoin, or we will be once they're worth a million dollars like everyone expects, we ought to put some of this unearned wealth to good use.*

Even then, Finney recognized Bitcoin's potential, estimating it could one day be worth $1 million. At the same time, he pointed to the opportunity—and perhaps even the responsibility that such an expansion would create: to use the wealth generated for good, for the betterment of society.

What exactly do Bitcoin's network effects look like?

With each additional user, the usefulness of Bitcoin increases for everyone else, either directly or indirectly. This increase in utility manifests as rising demand and, in turn, an increase in bitcoin's value. Who uses Bitcoin? There are four kinds of users: private individuals, businesses, governments, and perhaps even central banks.

If the first user of Bitcoin was the only user, it would have no value. Nothing could be done with it. Indeed, from its launch in January 2009 until approximately October 2009, bitcoin had no market value. The price was zero. Beginning in late 2009, the first transactions occurred, establishing a price for bitcoin in the range of a few U.S. cents. By the end of 2010, the price still had not exceeded about 30 cents.

The more companies that accept bitcoin, the more demand it creates among their customers. And the more customers who want to pay with bitcoin, the more worthwhile it becomes for businesses to accept it. At present, in El Salvador, for example, you can top up a prepaid SIM card with bitcoin via the Lightning Network in seconds and at virtually no cost. In Lugano, Switzerland, there are many shops that now accept bitcoin as a means of payment. The more users there are (in this case, companies and points of acceptance) the more useful it becomes for individuals to hold and use bitcoin for transactions. And the more people who hold bitcoin, the more worthwhile it is for shops and businesses to accept it—a self-affirming cycle.

Another direct network effect is that the more people or companies become familiar with Bitcoin, the easier it is for newcomers to learn about it. The more information there is available and the more accessible Bitcoin becomes, the easier it becomes to avoid technical errors while using it.

Indirect network effects in the Bitcoin ecosystem are diverse. The greater the number of users, the more complementary products emerge. For example, the number of YouTube channels, podcasts, and publications (including books and traditional media coverage) has grown significantly in recent years. The more knowledge is shared, the more users appear. And the more users there are, the greater the incentive to share knowledge, write a book, or create a new podcast.

It works similarly for developers. As more appear, so do more solutions that make Bitcoin easier to use and, in turn, increase adoption. A growing payment infrastructure, for example, now makes it very easy for merchants to accept, hold, or instantly convert bitcoin into a fiat currency with minimal exchange-rate risk. The more developers there are, the greater the range of bitcoin wallets and other solutions—and the better and more secure they become. Growing usage leads to more exchanges where bitcoin can be bought, which in turn attracts even more buyers when those exchanges market their products effectively. Even regulation, when well designed, can have a positive indirect network effect, because the more users there are, the more necessary regulation becomes. And well-executed regulation provides legal certainty, thereby encouraging further adoption.

At this point, three particularly strong self-affirming cycles are worth highlighting. Each of them can have both positive and negative effects.

The first is regulation. In early 2024, the U.S. SEC approved bitcoin ETFs. ETFs, or exchange-traded funds, are investment funds that track assets such as stocks, bonds, or commodities. They hold the underlying assets. For over a decade, various players, beginning with the Winklevoss brothers, have sought approval for a bitcoin ETF. Such a fund tracks the bitcoin price 1:1 by holding only bitcoin. This makes it possible to buy bitcoin through an ETF just like buying a stock. It allows access for investors who are deterred by technical hurdles or who are permitted to invest only in exchange-listed securities. An ETF, as a complementary financial product, increases access and, therefore, utility for buyers. The more ETFs there are, the more investors—especially institutional ones or users with limited technical skills—can buy bitcoin. The greater the demand for ETFs, the more of them will be offered. By early 2025, just about a year after approval, $40 billion had already been invested in the newly launched ETFs. By capital inflows, the BlackRock ETF was the most successful ETF launch.

The second cycle is price. Bitcoin's price can directly affect adoption, either positively or negatively. In so-called bull markets, i.e., phases in which the price rises sharply, Bitcoin attracts enormous amounts of attention. The media reports on it, and people brag about their gains at parties and gatherings. As prices rise, more people buy, which can create bubbles of various sizes. As soon as the price increase slows or a major price correction sets in, the reverse can occur: some investors sell as the price falls. The selling pushes the price down further, causing more investors to follow suit.

The third cycle is the computing power (hashrate) of the bitcoin miners. Bitcoin mining works through a randomized computational process where *hashes* (a special mathematical function) are calculated to determine who can add the next block to the blockchain and earn the block reward. Up to April 2024, that block reward was 6.25 bitcoin, then worth around $400,000. A new block is found, and its reward is generated approximately every ten minutes. Obviously, the payout can make mining very profitable; that's why miners are bringing more and more specialized machines online. The combined computing power of all bitcoin miners is known as the hashrate, and by early 2025, it was just under one zettahash, i.e., nearly 10^{21} hash calculations per second. A higher hashrate makes the Bitcoin network more secure by protecting it from attacks that could attempt to alter transactions already stored in the blockchain. The hashrate reflects the system's security and immutability.

The self-affirming cycle of the hashrate is particularly strong. The higher the hashrate, the more secure the Bitcoin network becomes and the greater its acceptance among new users. As acceptance increases, so does the price. A higher price, in turn, makes it more profitable to deploy additional machines for bitcoin mining. The hashrate then rises even further. This demonstrates how two cycles—price and hashrate—intertwine. When China expelled bitcoin miners from the country in May 2021, the network's hashrate sharply declined. This caused major uncertainty, sent the price of bitcoin down, and at least temporarily slowed the adoption of Bitcoin. The self-affirming cycle of "higher prices → more adoption → higher prices" flipped into reverse.

Overall, direct and indirect network effects both tend to be positive. They can, however, shift into reverse—at least temporarily—and have adverse effects. Their diversity has led to an overall positive effect so far, despite pauses and interruptions. The strongest and most enduringly positive effect on the Bitcoin network is the dilution of the conventional money supply, coupled with growing awareness of this. Bitcoin's intrinsic utility as a store of value, due to its fixed supply of 21 million coins, is so powerful in an inflationary environment that it can bridge temporarily negative network effects until they flip back to positive again.

Indirect network effects such as complementary products from developers, knowledge sharing, exchanges, favorable regulation, the ability to safely store bitcoin via service providers, high-performance hardware for miners or Bitcoin nodes, the hashrate, additional applications on the Bitcoin blockchain (so-called Layer-2 solutions), and development tools that integrate Bitcoin into existing products as well as other new use cases all lead to greater adoption and usage. This, in turn, reinforces the effect and the creation of new indirect network effects, and so the cycle continues.

What we observe here is a system that is becoming stronger and increasingly self-reinforcing. Utility and adoption continue to increase, as reflected in a steadily rising price, followed by further acceptance and popularity of Bitcoin. Although adoption remains low, often estimated at around 1–2% of the world's population, there's reason to believe that this process is only beginning and could continue to expand and intensify for many years to come.

The following figure provides a high-level overview of the various network components and feedback loops within the Bitcoin ecosystem. The plus signs denote self-affirming loops, which, as noted above, can also operate in reverse.

FIGURE 5 (p. 86): Various feedback loops describing the network effects that drive the adoption of Bitcoin by individuals, companies, and governments

The value that bitcoin can provide to companies can be significant. In the highly competitive market for top talent and developers, offering to pay part of the salary in bitcoin can make a decisive difference in recruiting. International payments can be processed more quickly and affordably. E-commerce businesses that accept it report larger shopping carts, fewer returns, and, of course, no payment defaults with bitcoin customers. In Germany, small

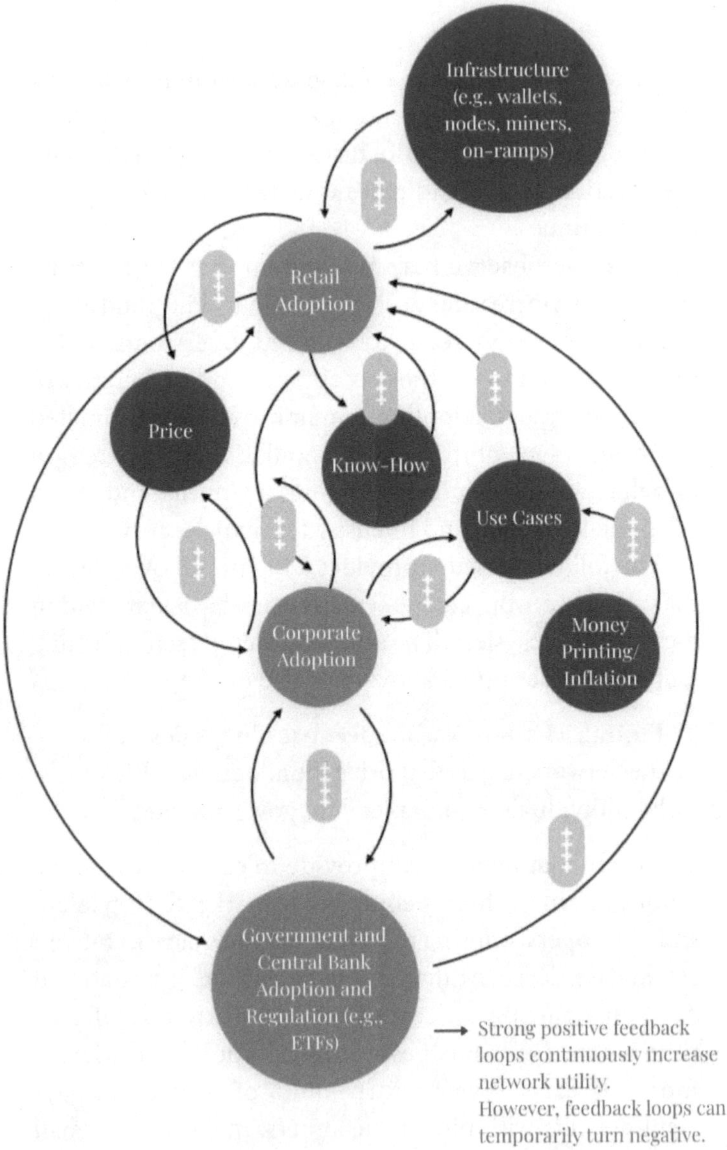

Source: Author's Illustration

amounts of bitcoin may be provided to employees tax-free as part of a benefits package. And if current trends continue as described, bitcoin could also make a meaningful contribution as a component of long-term retirement programs. Companies could invest unused cash reserves in bitcoin to protect against monetary devaluation. Strategy[B] (formerly MicroStrategy), for example, significantly boosted its share price through substantial bitcoin purchases beginning in August 2020 and even outperformed every company in the S&P 500 in 2024 (Strategy[B]'s and the business's use of bitcoin are discussed in more detail in Chapter 10).

To date, only one country—El Salvador—has adopted bitcoin as legal tender alongside the U.S. dollar. This was in 2021. Since then, the country has seen very positive developments. The economy is growing at an above-average rate, crime has decreased significantly, and tourism has increased considerably. Digital nomads are increasingly establishing operations in El Salvador, and companies such as Strike have relocated their headquarters there. The country's reputation has improved significantly. Bitcoin is part of a broader innovation and digitalization strategy that President Bukele is pursuing to modernize the country and enhance its security. It is true, however, that only part of El Salvador's positive progress since 2021 can be attributed to the adoption of bitcoin as legal tender and to its promotion through education.

Globally, central banks held around 37,000 tons of gold at the end of 2024. This corresponded to about €3 trillion in January 2025. Central banks hold gold as currency reserves that are independent of other fiat currencies, providing them with a form of insurance against major crises or financial system collapses. In principle, bitcoin and gold are similar. The key advantages of bitcoin are full self-custody and easy portability. Germany holds nearly half of its gold reserves, primarily in the United States, so that they can be sold quickly in an emergency. This undermines an entity's ability to access its own gold at any time. With bitcoin, there is no risk of being denied access. It is therefore conceivable that central banks may one day hold not only gold but also bitcoin in their currency reserves. While large-scale purchases of bitcoin by central banks may still seem unlikely today, a precedent could be set by younger and more forward-thinking leaders—similar to Bukele in El Salvador—who recognize the advantages of bitcoin, sell a portion of their gold, and acquire bitcoin instead. In Switzerland, for several years, there have been calls for the Swiss National Bank (SNB) to invest a portion of its vast currency reserves in bitcoin, and a popular initiative is currently underway to legally oblige the SNB to do so. As soon as one or more central banks take this step, others may feel compelled to follow suit.[14][15]

Another possible scenario is a central bank seeking to stabilize a depreciating currency by backing it with bitcoin. Using printed money, it could try to buy up as much bitcoin as possible and quite probably gain a near-insurmountable advantage over other central banks. After all, the number of bitcoin is limited. Depending on the willingness of the holders of the 19.9 million bitcoin in circulation as of

October 2025 to sell, it is conceivable that no single central bank would be able to acquire more than one million coins. Even if other central banks were subsequently willing to invest a lot of capital, they would very likely only be able to accumulate a comparatively small amount, as the willingness to sell among current bitcoin holders might be low, and it's often estimated that only six to nine million bitcoin are available for sale at all.

The fascinating thing about Bitcoin technology is that the value of its network is reflected directly in its price. By owning a share of bitcoin, you own a part of the network itself. The more the network spreads, the more applications emerge beyond being a store of value; the more diverse and stronger the resulting network effects, the sooner the Bitcoin network establishes itself as a de facto standard, and ultimately, the more valuable the network and bitcoin become. Virtually anyone with internet access also has access to Bitcoin, so there are roughly six billion people worldwide who could be potential users.

Chapter 10:

Company Adoption: Michael Saylor and Strategy[B] (formerly MicroStrategy)

When Michael Saylor announced on August 10, 2020, that he had purchased 21,454 bitcoin for $250 million, the world was stunned. In the midst of the COVID-19 crisis, when it was still unclear whether the world might completely collapse, Saylor was the first CEO of a publicly traded company to convert dollars into bitcoin. This first purchase was made at a bitcoin price of $11,650.

It may be a coincidence, but Saylor's extensive bitcoin purchases were soon followed by the 2021 bull market, which would drive bitcoin up to $69,000 in November 2021.

Saylor is first and foremost an entrepreneur. In 1989, he founded MicroStrategy in Vienna, Virginia. Among other things, the company focuses on business intelligence, which is the analysis of data to generate insights for enterprises. Following its 1998 IPO, the company grew modestly, with $500 million in revenue in 2022.

In his 2012 book, *The Mobile Wave: How Mobile Intelligence Will Change Everything*, Saylor foresaw, with remarkable precision, the impact of mobile computing on society in general and on business in particular. This was followed by highly successful private investments in companies such as Apple and Facebook, both of which benefited substantially from these trends.

Like so many others, Saylor used the downtime created by the initial pandemic lockdowns to delve into bitcoin. If the COVID-19 pandemic had a silver lining, it was that many people used their unexpected free time to explore new subjects. COVID-19 forced countless people to change long-entrenched habits. This combination of extra time, the pressure to change, and the massive money printing that was being done by governments and central banks formed the cocktail of events that led many to bitcoin.

Saylor has since gained worldwide recognition for his extraordinary financial commitment and his extreme conviction about Bitcoin. By October 2025, he had acquired 640,808 bitcoin for Strategy[B] at an average price of about $74,000, a total investment of an astounding $47 billion. Saylor has underlined this commitment with outspoken and conviction-filled public appearances in which he repeatedly points out how monetary expansion dilutes the dollar, significantly eroding its purchasing power, especially in the long term, and effectively dispossessing the general population. One of his core messages is that no other asset or cryptocurrency comes close to bitcoin: *There is no second best.*

Through his extraordinary financial commitment, the subsequent strong performance of Strategy^{B}'s share price (which, from the first bitcoin purchase in August 2020 until August 2024, outperformed all other stocks in the S&P 500), and his unbridled confidence in bitcoin's long-term success, Saylor has generated enormous attention for Bitcoin. Since those first purchases in August 2020, Strategy^{B}'s stock price—albeit with some significant fluctuations—has increased about fiftyfold.

Beyond using bitcoin as a store of value, Saylor has also integrated it into Strategy^{B}'s business processes. He pays himself, the other board members, and the supervisory board members in Bitcoin, and offers the same option to the company's employees. The resulting attention and the ability to attract highly sought-after talent in the *War for Talent* have had a positive impact on Strategy^{B}'s business development.

What value does Bitcoin create for businesses?

The impact of Bitcoin on a company is crucial to further corporate adoption. Michael Saylor sees bitcoin as a store of value. Surplus cash that one does not want to see devalued by inflation can be parked in bitcoin. He stresses that doing so requires a long-term perspective. Funds parked in bitcoin should not be needed for at least four years. He has supplemented these purchases with both debt-financed and equity-financed acquisitions. He offers investors financial products—convertible notes, Strategy^{B} shares, and, more recently, preferred shares—so that they can profit from bitcoin. This is particularly relevant for investors who cannot buy bitcoin directly. Convertible notes offer reduced risk with below-average nominal yields but significant upside through conversion, while shares provide an above-average risk/reward profile compared to buying bitcoin directly.

Another obvious use case is employing bitcoin for payments. Bitcoin payments can be considerably faster and much cheaper than payments in traditional fiat currencies. Transferring money across the globe to a country with weak payment infrastructure can be tedious and expensive. However, selling products in exchange for bitcoin, especially via the Lightning Network, incurs significantly lower fees than, for example, credit card payments. Credit card payments take about two months to be fully processed, during which time incoming payments can still be reversed (chargebacks). A bitcoin payment, by contrast, is finalized after about ten minutes, and a Lightning payment is instantly final. Many e-commerce companies experience average payment defaults of 1–2%. A bitcoin payment, once made, is practically irreversible, even with just a single block confirmation. Offering a bitcoin payment option could also help reach a potentially more affluent customer base. One e-commerce company I know reports significantly larger shopping carts and fewer returns when customers pay with bitcoin.

The offer to pay a portion of the salary in bitcoin can be beneficial, particularly for enterprises recruiting highly specialized technical talent. The company not only enhances its image as highly innovative but also attracts relevant expertise in bitcoin. This could be of particular interest to banks, for example, that want to integrate the option to buy bitcoin into their online banking services. Surprisingly, as of January 2025, a number of Swiss banks already offer this, while in Germany, only neobanks do, and none of the traditional banks.

Once a company has invested a portion of its reserves in bitcoin, those reserves can serve as collateral for short-, medium-, or long-term loans. Using them in this manner avoids a potentially taxable sale of the bitcoin while retaining the possibility of further price appreciation. A company called Firefish.io, based in Prague, facilitates peer-to-peer loans that are secured by bitcoin. Within a few hours, you can find a lender by offering your bitcoin as collateral. Swiss banks that offer bitcoin purchases also grant securities-backed or Lombard loans by accepting bitcoin as collateral.

Within the scope of corporate energy management, Bitcoin mining can be used to utilize surplus electricity, for instance, under fixed purchase agreements or in-house solar installations. Mining also generates heat, as with any data center, and this waste heat could be reused in a facility's heating systems.

Strategy[B] and several other companies are pursuing the approach of integrating Bitcoin into existing products and developing new business models. Through the Lightning Network, continuous micropayments at sub-cent levels are enabled. When a product or service is used, payment can flow over the Lightning Network in real time—even for very short usage periods—creating a newly feasible version of the pay-per-use model.

At present, the circle of companies adopting Bitcoin has expanded significantly. These include some publicly traded firms such as Semler Scientific, Marathon Digital Holdings, the Japanese company Metaplanet, the French company The Blockchain Group, and even Tesla and Block. In Germany, several medium-sized companies have adopted Bitcoin; for example, through Volksbank Bayern Mitte. That said, these companies refrain from aggressive public appearances. To date, Strategy[B] has made the most extensive purchases.

It is quite clear that Bitcoin can provide companies with a wide variety of benefits. Beyond simply preserving the value of money issued in inflationary periods, bitcoin can also improve a company's operational performance. It's only a matter of time before many more businesses discover and act on this potential.

Chapter 11: El Salvador and Bhutan—Country Adoption

Until a few years ago, El Salvador was characterized by extreme poverty, persistently high crime rates, and, since the end of the civil war in 1992, successive governments that were more focused on their own interests than the well-being of their people.

That started to change in 2019, when Nayib Bukele was elected president, at just thirty-eight years old and as an outsider, with an absolute majority. He has since been consistently implementing a modernization and digitization strategy. Through sometimes unconventional and controversial measures, he has continued the crime-reduction strategy he initiated during his tenure as mayor of San Salvador, the capital of El Salvador.

Bukele and El Salvador gained worldwide attention in June 2021, when he announced, and later implemented in September 2021, the introduction of bitcoin as legal tender alongside the U.S. dollar. Since 2001, El Salvador no

longer had its own currency and has exclusively used the U.S. dollar.

Without delving further into the country's history, Bukele's policies can be viewed as a serious alternative to administrations characterized by war, rampant crime, and self-enrichment at the expense of the general population. Perhaps Bukele is following in the tradition of his predecessors and is only doing it for his own benefit and enrichment—or perhaps it is a genuine attempt to give a beleaguered population a lasting chance of a better standard of living.

In a widely noted tweet in June 2021 that was retweeted by Bukele, I summed it up as follows:

Alex v. Frankenberg (Hodltrainer)
@Justdoitalex

In case we see a significant improvement in El Salvador's economic performance, crime rate, standard of living in a few years, the world will be on a #bitcoin ₿ standard in the 2030s. And #bitcoin ₿ will hit 10 million USD easily.

Post übersetzen

7:29 nachm. · 6. Juni 2021 aus Bonn, Deutschland

Post-Statistiken anzeigen

219 Reposts **6** Zitate **1.521** „Gefällt mir"-Angaben **11** Lesezeichen

If the adoption and integration of Bitcoin, alongside other measures, help improve the lives of Salvadorans, then other countries could follow, bringing correspondingly positive effects on the value of the Bitcoin network and on Bitcoin itself.

By August 2024, Bukele had succeeded in sharply reducing the crime rate, particularly the nation's very high homicide rate. Officially, El Salvador's rate of two murders per 100,000 inhabitants is now lower than that of the United States. This was achieved through the relentless pursuit, disarmament, and arrest of gangs and other criminals. In parallel, Bukele has pursued a modernization and digitization strategy. For example, every student has been equipped with a laptop. Part of this innovation strategy is the introduction of bitcoin as a second legal tender.

The results are mixed but positive overall. Crime has fallen sharply, and the economy is on a solid upward trajectory. The country's image has greatly improved, with tourism on the rise and an increased influx of digital nomads and companies. In September 2024, Bukele even announced a buyback of part of the country's outstanding national debt. This economic upturn has significantly improved El Salvador's financial position.

The adoption of Bitcoin, however, has fallen far short of expectations. Only a small portion of remittance payments sent home by El Salvadorans living in the U.S. are currently processed in bitcoin or via the Lightning Network, for example. The high transaction fees charged by established financial institutions, roughly $400 million annually, which could in principle be avoided by using bitcoin, are still being paid. Although numerous merchants in the capital and other major cities now accept bitcoin, it has not yet gained traction among the broader population.

Chapter 11

Contrary to expectations, other countries have not yet followed El Salvador's lead. Bitcoin's notorious volatility, particularly its sharp price decline in 2022, has been a contributing factor. Although long-term cycles show a stable upward trend, politicians focused on short-term outcomes are unable to recognize this and withstand the downward fluctuations. As of early 2025, bitcoin is no longer a mandatory legal tender in El Salvador. Although the government continues to purchase one bitcoin per day and encourages its adoption, it no longer requires businesses and merchants to accept the cryptocurrency.

Just as bitcoin is not a cure-all for an individual's shaky finances, flawed strategy, or failing business model, it is also not a quick fix for the numerous challenges faced by societies and nations. El Salvador nonetheless remains a notable experiment for nation-states to observe. In a country that had almost nothing left to lose—and in the context of a broader digitization and innovation push, sound economic and fiscal policies, and a major improvement in domestic security—Bitcoin could bring many positive effects that play out across multiple levels over the medium- and long-term. After all, Bukele's policies, with Bitcoin as one component, have contributed to considerable optimism and positive energy in El Salvador, as well as record-high approval ratings and the president's re-election.

The small Himalayan kingdom of Bhutan suddenly appeared on Bitcoiners' radars when information about its Bitcoin activities emerged in connection with the Celsius bankruptcy. It wasn't until the summer of 2024 that more concrete details emerged about Bhutan's activities and its bitcoin holdings. The story is similar to El Salvador's: a poor country trying to pull itself up by its own bootstraps.[16]

Bhutan's fifth king, Jigme Khesar Namgyel Wangchuck, apparently discovered and understood Bitcoin around 2011. In a personal conversation at the Bhutan Innovation Forum in early October 2024, he summarized his Bitcoin strategy to me in three words: *Hodl, hodl, hodl.* Later conversations revealed a more nuanced strategy. In Bhutan, too, Bitcoin serves a variety of purposes.

One of Bhutan's key assets is an abundance of low-cost, renewable energy. Ample rainfall and numerous towering mountains have enabled Bhutan to develop abundant hydropower. Electricity is the nation's primary export, sold to India. Since 2019, however, Bhutan has also diverted a small portion of this cheap, clean electricity into Bitcoin mining and building national wealth in the process.

As of January 2025, Bhutan officially held 13,000 bitcoin, equivalent to about 1.3 billion U.S. dollars. At around 50% of its GNP, Bhutan's bitcoin holdings are the largest in the world relative to the size of its economy. That works out to just under 0.02 bitcoin per capita, or the equivalent of about fifteen months' average wages for each citizen. Depending on future pricing and continued mining, it's foreseeable that the value of Bhutan's bitcoin holdings could exceed its GNP of roughly $3 billion in the coming years.

Bhutan sells off only a small portion of the Bitcoin it mines. One reason is to import electricity from India during the winter, when reduced rainfall reduces hydropower generation. In this sense, Bitcoin indirectly serves as a battery for Bhutan's energy system. Bhutan also occasionally sells a tiny fraction of its Bitcoin holdings when it is in urgent need of foreign currency.

Bhutan now has the capability to build and maintain its own extensive mining facilities. This facility can also be used to earn money elsewhere. Building on this foundation, the kingdom plans to expand into further technical skill sets. Notably, Bhutan is the only country in the world to have developed a blockchain-based national ID card. Approximately 20% of the population already uses it, providing them with seamless access to various government services. They can also authorize its use for other purposes; for example, they can selectively disclose their personal data for further processing.

As in El Salvador, Bitcoin is not a panacea for all of Bhutan's challenges. But it is one element of a very long-term modernization strategy that also aims to preserve the country's traditions and cultural values. Bitcoin is quite compatible with the nation's Buddhist ethos. It utilizes Bhutan's natural resources, supports harmony between people and nature, and offers a long-term positive outlook.

Is bitcoin a rival to traditional fiat currencies?

Until 1971, fiat currencies were at least partially backed by gold. Gold served as an anchor, restraining the expansion of the money supply. On August 15, 1971, in his now-famous address, U.S. President Richard Nixon temporarily suspended the convertibility of gold into the U.S. dollar. Since then, the dollar's devaluation has accelerated.

The website wtfhappenedin1971.com vividly illustrates the various effects that have accompanied this erosion of the dollar.[17]

One widely discussed idea is to back fiat currencies with bitcoin, thereby supporting them. The strength of the Swiss franc is attributable not only to the Swiss government's solid fiscal management but also to the Swiss National Bank's robust balance sheet, which held currency reserves of approximately F725 billion in 2023. At that time, gold accounted for only 58 billion francs of this total, playing a relatively minor role. The lion's share of 655 billion francs was made up of investments in bonds and stocks. Although the stock portion of these currency reserves is more volatile, it forms a solid backing for the Swiss franc.[18]

It would be a simple matter to directly invest a portion of these reserves in bitcoin. Indirectly, the Swiss National Bank already holds bitcoin through its investments in Strategy[B]. But if it were to hold bitcoin directly, the National Bank would have complete control of the bitcoin through its private keys and could transfer or sell it at any time if necessary. Unlike with gold, authenticity is automatically guaranteed by the blockchain. Diversifying currency reserves into bitcoin would not only enhance central banks' capacity to act but also reduce the costs of storage and transactions. Instead of being transported across the globe under high security, bitcoin could be transferred instantly via the blockchain.

And based on past performance, bitcoin could positively influence the value development of the currency reserves.

Dr. Luzius Meisser presented this in detail at the Swiss National Bank's General Meeting in April 2024, repeatedly suggesting that the bank should purchase bitcoin. If it makes sense for Switzerland, it makes sense for all 193 countries worldwide.

Since the freezing of Russia's currency reserves as a reaction to its war with Ukraine, many countries have increased their gold reserves. For instance, Saudi Arabia recently bought about 160 tons, while China may have purchased as much as 1,000 tons. The precise motives are rarely disclosed. It could simply be normal diversification, perhaps a hedge against inflation in times of rising prices, or maybe a safeguard against the seizure of fiat currency reserves. Any of these reasons would likewise justify purchasing bitcoin.[19]

It is only a matter of time before a country either buys bitcoin in significant quantities or publicly announces that such purchases have already been made. In Venezuela, the opposition to the current government has announced its intention to do so should it come to power. The same was said by the presidential candidate for Suriname, Maya Parbhoe. During his campaign, President Donald Trump repeatedly advocated for creating a strategic bitcoin reserve, envisioned to comprise approximately one million bitcoin.

If adding bitcoin to currency reserves proves successful in strengthening and stabilizing a country's fiat currency and its financial system, it is clear that one country after another will follow suit. Even a modest addition of bitcoin alongside existing gold reserves would have a significant impact on Bitcoin's broader adoption and, as a result, its price.

Chapter 12:
How Should You Buy Bitcoin?

The best and most obvious strategy in the past was simple: you just bought it. Assuming the price will rise, the best buying strategy is to put every euro you can spare for savings over the coming years into bitcoin—unless you see other investment opportunities that are similarly lucrative. This chapter is not about the best ways to buy or most securely store acquired bitcoin, however. It's about the amount and timing of purchases; first, how much, and then how often.

How much bitcoin should you buy?

In a famous quote from January 17, 2009, Satoshi Nakamoto simply recommended buying some bitcoin, just in case it caught on:

> *It might make sense to get some in case it catches on. If enough people think the same way, that becomes a self-fulfilling prophecy.*

It's true; if enough people share this opinion, it becomes a reality. Trust in Bitcoin, as well as increasing acceptance and usage, are central to its success. Gold, for instance, has intrinsic value as jewelry and as an industrial metal.[20] As with fiat currencies, there is no intrinsic value in bitcoin. If enough people share the opinion that it has value, it becomes valuable.

But even major skeptics might consider buying a small amount of bitcoin, because you never know what might happen. What do I mean by a *small amount*? Perhaps 1% of your savings or half of your monthly savings. Losing that amount might sting, but it wouldn't ruin you financially. Even if you invested only 5% of your savings, you'd only be risking the equivalent of an average annual return from a well-invested stock portfolio.

You could also set a specific bitcoin target. The absolute minimum might be 0.002625 bitcoin, i.e., the per capita share of the total supply if it were distributed equally worldwide.[21] Other goals could include 0.1 bitcoin, half a bitcoin, a full bitcoin, or even the equivalent of one year's net salary.

How much you invest depends on the following important factors, including how strongly you believe in the ongoing inflation of fiat currencies and the fragility of the financial system, how confident you are in Bitcoin's long-term prospects for success, and how much stress you can handle from the volatility that repeatedly occurs and often lasts for extended periods. A good rule of thumb is that if you can no longer sleep well at night, you've bought too much bitcoin.

Once you've settled on an amount you want to invest, the question is how to invest it—either all at once or spread out over time.

If you're convinced bitcoin's price is about to rise, it would make sense to invest in one go, because it'll only get more expensive if your investment is spread out. However, if you expect the price to fall in the future, it might be better to buy at least a portion later on.

The following diagrams illustrate the outcomes of a single lump-sum purchase versus repeated smaller purchases over time, known as dollar-cost averaging (DCA), in a scenario in which an initial drop in the bitcoin price is followed by a recovery.

For example, suppose the starting price for 1 bitcoin is €100,000. You invest €100,000; the price falls to €40,000 (a 60% decline) and then rises back to €100,000. After thirteen months, the price is back where it began.

With a lump-sum purchase, your maximum (unrealized) loss is 60%. At the end of the period, your loss is zero. You still hold 1 bitcoin.

With dollar-cost averaging, you allocate the total amount to thirteen monthly investments of approximately €7,700. By the end of the investment period, you've invested €100,000, as in the first example.

Figure 6 (p. 110): The profit trajectory (in light gray) comparing lump-sum purchases with dollar-cost averaging (DCA).

Dollar-Cost Averaging Can Lead to Higher Returns Due to Bitcoin's Volatility

Lump-Sum Purchase

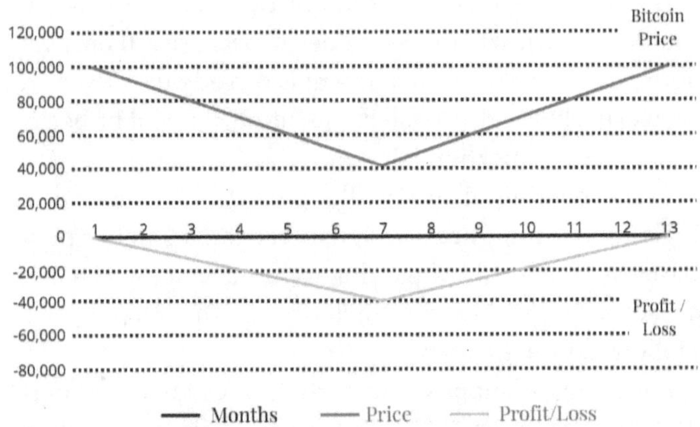

Dollar-Cost Averaging

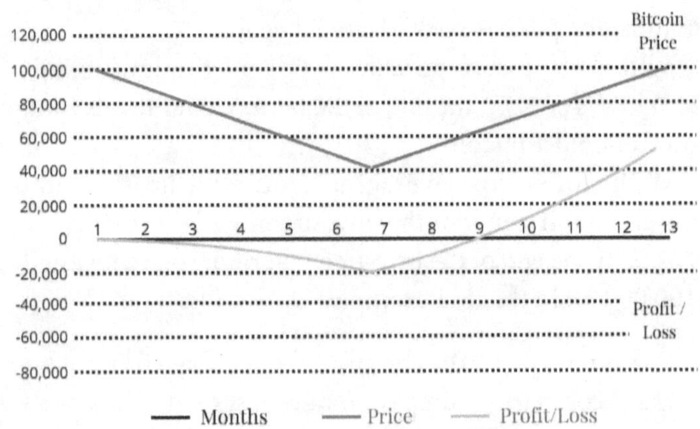

Source: Author's Illustration

What is important is the trajectory. Even with a price drop of 60%, your maximum loss with DCA is only €20,000—obviously much less than with a lump-sum purchase. Even more important is that when prices fall and you invest a fixed amount, you end up buying more bitcoin. This results in you end the period with 1.5 bitcoin and a €50,000 profit.

In other words, you get more bitcoin if you invest fixed amounts regularly and the price falls for a certain period. Most importantly, you will be less stressed because the maximum loss is reduced by two-thirds (€20,000 instead of €60,000). If stress leads you to sell all your bitcoin in frustration, you end up with only €40,000 from the lump-sum purchase and no bitcoin, whereas with dollar-cost averaging, you would have 1.5 bitcoin worth €150,000. This is clearly the superior buying strategy. A bitcoin savings plan with small, regular purchases causes far less stress and encourages long-term thinking.

I have also developed a third strategy: buying small amounts on specific occasions, repeatedly, little by little. Here's an example. In the fall of 2021, I was on a train from Hamburg to Bonn, scheduled to take approximately 4.5 hours. As usual, the train was late, but this time significantly more than usual, about five hours late. I wasn't going to get home until 1:30 in the morning. On the train, after I finished answering all my emails and messages during the journey home, I decided to treat myself to a beer from the onboard bistro. Unfortunately, it was closed. Instead of getting even more annoyed with the situation, I decided to buy bitcoin with the money I would have spent on the beer. It would probably have been three beers, so I bought €15 worth of bitcoin.

On an especially good day, I might buy €10 worth of bitcoin. On a really bad day, €20. It instantly makes me feel much better.

For many years, I've abstained from drinking alcohol for the first three months of the year. That saves quite a bit of money, which I then use to buy bitcoin. Another really great occasion to buy is when leading economists or ECB directors proclaim that the money supply has no effect on inflation—just like that, I've bought a few more euros' worth of bitcoin. Or when politicians describe debt as an asset. Yet another few satoshis in the wallet. (A *satoshi*, named after Bitcoin's creator, is the smallest available unit of bitcoin.)

The online bank Revolut offers a feature that rounds up every payment you make and automatically buys bitcoin with the difference. Those bitcoin can now be transferred to your own wallet. Various credit card providers also offer cashback programs in which cardholders earn cash back when using the card. Satsback.com is one such service; instead of cashback in fiat, you receive satoshis sent directly to your Lightning wallet. Several online shops are partners of Satsback. This means when you shop via Satsback.com, you receive small amounts of bitcoin paid directly into a wallet as cashback.

You hardly notice (or maybe don't notice at all) when you buy bitcoin in small, regular amounts. But it adds up.

Then suddenly, after a few years, you find yourself holding a meaningful amount of bitcoin, made even more valuable by price appreciation. And let's face it, we were going to skip that last beer anyway.

Section 4:
Satoshi Nakamoto
and the Technology

THE TIMES
Chancelor on brink of
second bailout for banks

Chapter 13:
Decoding Satoshi Nakamoto

Hopefully, we will never find out who is behind the pseudonym *Satoshi Nakamoto.* No one knows who actually created Bitcoin, or even whether it was a single individual or a small group of people. We don't know whether it was a private initiative or, as some have speculated, a government or even an intelligence agency. We don't know the nationality or regional origin of Bitcoin either. It's very likely that the obvious *clues,* like the Japanese name *Satoshi Nakamoto* and the British English writing style used in the white paper, were carefully chosen to conceal the true origin of Bitcoin.

It is precisely this anonymity, this lack of personal and regional ties, that is central to Bitcoin's distinctive character—a decentralized system that cannot be controlled or altered by any central authority. Bitcoin simply exists. It lives on its own, imposes itself on no one, and is open to everyone. No one has to use it, but anyone can. Bitcoin exists beyond societies, beyond the fiat system—it is apolitical and resistant to manipulation. Bitcoin has no agenda and no goal. It simply exists with its unique properties.

Bitcoin says, "Here I am. Whoever sees the benefits and wants them is free to use me."

The absence of a central figure or entity that created Bitcoin makes this complete decentralization possible. It is also the key difference between it and almost all other blockchain-based systems. There is nearly always a controlling group that has set the rules—and therefore can also change them. As such, there is always the possibility, or at least the temptation, to adjust these systems for either the common good or personal gain. For example, money is printed to stabilize the economy during a crisis, such as COVID-19, or to protect citizens from rising energy prices. Similarly, in other cryptocurrencies and blockchains, the rules governing the quantity or extent to which new coins are created can be changed relatively easily.

Bitcoin's decentralization is unique. It ensures the limit of 21 million bitcoin, prevents inflation beyond that limit, and thus makes bitcoin a historically unique store of value. The decision by Bitcoin's creator or creators (who operate under the pseudonym *Satoshi Nakamoto*) to remain anonymous—to forgo fame, recognition, and even the roughly 1 million coins mined in the early days—is central to its long-term success. This anonymity acts as the final piece of the puzzle that perfects the system. That system has now been established for over seventeen years, and Bitcoin has built such powerful network effects (see Chapter 9) that it is virtually impossible for any new alternative to surpass it.

Bitcoin was a direct response to the 2007–2009 financial crisis, which nearly led to the collapse of the global financial system. Even fundamentally sound companies like Goldman Sachs could not have survived the impending collapse without the hundreds of billions of dollars in newly created money that the U.S. government and, in particular, the U.S. Federal Reserve poured into rescuing the financial system. The response to an unsound financial system was to print money and inflate.

Numerous clues left by the developer or developers who worked under the pseudonym Satoshi Nakamoto show their intention to establish bitcoin as an alternative to an ever-inflating fiat system.

Date of the white paper: October 31, 2008.

On October 31, 1517, the Augustinian friar Martin Luther nailed his 95 Theses against the sale of letters of indulgence to the door of Castle Church in Wittenberg. According to traditional interpretation, this marked the beginning of the Reformation, the separation of church and state.

Letters of indulgence were sold by the church to believers under the premise that they would free their souls from eternal purgatory. What the letters actually did was take money from those who wanted their sins absolved and transfer it to the church. Satoshi draws a parallel to these letters. In today's financial system, inflation erodes the purchasing power of citizens' hard-earned money by steadily eroding its value. The letters of indulgence took people's money away without providing anything in return. Martin Luther was concerned with the separation of church and state. Satoshi Nakamoto was concerned with the separation of money and state.

Timing: Bitcoin appeared at the peak of the financial crisis. In October 2008, the global financial system teetered on the brink of collapse. The bankruptcy of Lehman Brothers on September 15, 2008, triggered widespread failures across the financial sector. Banks no longer trusted one another, refinancing dried up, and they were nearly all on the verge of collapse. It was only through massive, coordinated interventions by central banks and governments that this total collapse was narrowly averted.

Launch of the Bitcoin blockchain and the first block: January 3, 2009.

It is possible to embed short text messages directly into Bitcoin blocks, where they're preserved forever. The very first block quotes a January 3, 2009, headline from *The Times: "Chancellor on Brink of Second Bailout for Banks."* On that day, a second bailout package for British banks had become necessary. Satoshi's choice to embed that headline in the genesis block was a deliberate commentary on the failures of the financial system.

Satoshi Nakamoto's birthday: April 5, 1975.

Just like the name of the character Satoshi Nakamoto, his birth date is also fictitious. Satoshi listed it as April 5, 1975.

On April 5, 1933, U.S. President Franklin D. Roosevelt issued Executive Order 6102, mandating that all private citizens in the United States hand over their gold holdings to the government. Gold was confiscated in exchange for what was, in retrospect, clearly insufficient compensation of $20 per ounce, and stripped of its status as legal tender. One year later, in 1934, the official price of gold was raised to $35 per ounce, thereby expropriating the original holders. This prohibition of gold ownership was part of a long tradition of bans on gold and served to enable further monetary expansion beyond the limits imposed by gold backing. By banning gold, the American government had denied its citizens the ability to escape an inflationary system that was expropriating them. Similar patterns are observed in nearly all high-inflation countries. Foreign currency holdings are prohibited or at least heavily restricted. In Argentina, U.S. dollar holdings have repeatedly been forcibly converted. With inflation running at approximately 50% per month until Javier Milei took office in December 2023, Argentinian citizens were deprived of the opportunity to protect their money against significant devaluation.[22]

Satoshi Nakamoto's chosen birth date, April 5, clearly references the April 5, 1933, gold ban. Even gold, which lies outside the financial system and carries no counterparty risk, is not suitable as a store of value if it can be banned or ultimately expropriated. Bitcoin, by contrast, could also be banned; however, as long as access is controlled by a private key, it cannot be seized. Gold's physical properties also make it difficult to transport or to hide beyond a small quantity. Even small amounts of gold can be detected by vigilant border control officers. A metal detector will certainly find it, no matter where it's hidden. Bitcoin, however, is digital. If there's an emergency, a private key or seed phrase can simply be memorized and transported across a border in one's own head. You could literally walk naked across a border and still carry your entire fortune to another country with Bitcoin. No one would know. This is impossible with all other assets.

Private gold ownership in the U.S. was only legalized again in 1975, four years after Nixon had officially (though *temporarily*) suspended the dollar's convertibility into gold. So, Satoshi Nakamoto's chosen birthday symbolizes both the beginning and the end of the gold ban in the United States.

21 million bitcoin

Why is bitcoin limited to exactly 21 million? Why not 17 million, or 63 million, or 200 million? The specific number of possible bitcoin is completely irrelevant to the system, its functionality, and the underlying intention.

In 2017, I was wondering how much money actually exists in the world, specifically in the M1 money supply. M1 includes cash in circulation and money in accounts that are available on demand, such as checking accounts. At the time, I discovered that the global M1 money supply in 2008 was around $21 trillion, according to the CIA World Factbook. While conducting research for this book, I was unable to locate the source again. I only found the figures of $30.1 trillion at the end of 2016 and $34.4 trillion at the end of 2017. [23]

If you assume the 2008 global M1 money supply was $21 trillion and convert it to cents, you obtain 2,100 trillion U.S. cents. While dollars are divided into cents, bitcoin is divided into satoshis, with one bitcoin equal to 100 million satoshis. Multiply the 21 million bitcoin by these satoshis, and you get the same number: 2,100 trillion satoshis. That is the same number as the global M1 money supply in 2008, measured in cents.

This could be a pure coincidence, or it could be an intended statement. The vision may have been that bitcoin could eventually replace the 2008 global M1 money supply. That would also correspond to a value of 1 U.S. cent per Satoshi, or $1 million per bitcoin in the monetary value of that time. The late computer programmer Hal Finney (who received the first-ever bitcoin transaction from Satoshi Nakamoto and might have been part of the early developer group) had already mentioned back in 2011—when bitcoin was priced at under $1—that a future price of $1 million was conceivable.

Both the growth of the money supply since 2008, particularly during the crises that followed the global financial crisis, and bitcoin's link to the 2008 M1 supply underscore the importance of bitcoin as an undilutable asset and its potential for value appreciation.

Chapter 14:
The Technology

At its core, the Bitcoin blockchain is nothing more than a database with novel properties. Bitcoin is a part of this database.

Bitcoin is transparent. The software that powers the system is open source, and the database is organized in a decentralized way. No one has the ability to simply make changes. The creation of new bitcoin is set in the software. On average, new coins are created every ten minutes. The total supply of bitcoin is capped at 21 million. This makes bitcoin permanently undilutable—a system that is decentralized, immutable, open source, and finite. There is no central authority you must put your trust in. The trust lies in the software and the decentralized network.

Satoshi Nakamoto addressed the point of scarcity and decentralization in a now-famous statement.

> *The root problem with conventional currency is all the trust that's required to make it work. The central bank must be trusted not to debase the*

> *currency, but the history of fiat currencies is full of breaches of that trust.*

The trust in Bitcoin is fundamentally ensured by three decentralized groups: nodes, miners, and core developers. The nodes run on very simple, inexpensive computers that host distributed copies of the blockchain. Each node stores its own independent copy and verifies its correctness. Any change, i.e., a new entry into the database, must adhere to the rules as defined in the Bitcoin software. If not, the nodes will reject it. As of October 2024, there were nearly 20,000 nodes.[24]

Then there are the miners, who compete for the opportunity to add pending transactions to the blockchain. This happens on average every ten minutes. Transactions are grouped into blocks, which are appended to the blockchain. When a miner successfully adds a block, it receives two rewards. One is the block reward, currently 3.125 bitcoin, which is newly created, and the other consists of transaction fees. Whether a miner can add a new block to the blockchain depends on solving a highly complex mathematical puzzle. The first to solve it can attach the block to the blockchain and thereby earn the reward. Because solving the puzzle is extremely computationally intensive and therefore costly, miners are strongly incentivized to be honest and comply with the rules to obtain the reward. If they do not adhere to the rules set in the software, nodes will reject their block. In that case, the miner would incur the costs but receive no reward.

Chapter 14

The Bitcoin software is maintained by a group of Bitcoin Core developers, who update it cautiously; typically, there is only one major update per year. Even the developers cannot impose unilateral changes. For example, if they attempted to modify the software by increasing the 21 million cap, the nodes would reject the change.

For the first time in history, Satoshi Nakamoto has created a decentralized system that all participants can trust. And for the first time, this trust requires no central authority. With Bitcoin as part of this system, a digital asset has emerged that cannot be copied. It can be transferred, but once it changes hands, the sender no longer has access to it. This is also historically unique. Previously, digital goods could be infinitely multiplied. This replicability was the defining feature of both the printing press and the internet.

New bitcoin are created through new blocks that are added to the blockchain. Two mechanisms regulate this process. The software adjusts the difficulty of solving the puzzle for a new block to ensure that, on average, a new block is created every ten minutes. If the miners' computing power increases, causing new blocks to be created faster, the software increases the difficulty to maintain the ten-minute average; conversely, if the miners' computing power decreases, the software decreases the difficulty to maintain the ten-minute average. In addition, the amount of new bitcoin issued as a reward for finding a block is halved every 210,000 blocks, approximately every four years. Initially, 50 bitcoin were awarded per block. This was halved to 25 bitcoin in 2012, to 12.5 bitcoin in 2016, to 6.25 bitcoin in

2020, and to 3.125 bitcoin in April 2024. This halving will occur 32 times, until around 2140, when no new coins will be issued. The maximum supply of just under 21 million bitcoin will then be reached. From that point on, miners will only receive the transaction fees as their reward.

The software is open source, so anyone can view and access it. It can easily be copied, and the copies can also be modified. Any parameter, such as the total supply or the average time required for a new block to be written, can be readily altered. In fact, this has happened dozens of times. Such a new copy of the system, known as a hard fork, has no impact on the main Bitcoin network so long as none or only a few follow the new system.

In 2017, a fork of the Bitcoin network, Bitcoin Cash, failed spectacularly, as described in Jonathan Bier's The *Blocksize War: The Battle for Control over Bitcoin's Protocol Rules*. The technology itself can readily be altered or improved. But unless the networks—that is, the nodes, miners, and core developers of the Bitcoin technology—choose to adopt the new changes, no new system is created. Dozens of such changes or forks have been attempted, so far, always unsuccessfully. Today, the combined market value of all bitcoin copies is less than 1% of bitcoin's value. The key to understanding Bitcoin's technology is this: it's not just about the code itself, but about the interplay of the network of nodes, miners, and core developers.[25]

Chapter 15:
Bitcoin—The Internet of Value

The internet is ancient, in digital terms. As early as the 1960s, precursors to the internet emerged when the U.S. military linked a handful of computers across the country. At that time, the general public had no access to it.

In the 1980s, the first widely usable precursors of the internet appeared: Bildschirmtext (BTX) and, later, CompuServe and AOL. These were proprietary solutions that, while open in the sense that anyone could join, were still closed-off worlds of their own. If you wanted to communicate with someone, that person had to be part of the same network. As recently as the early 1990s, an email within CompuServe to another CompuServe user was free, but an email to an internet address cost 10 U.S. cents. Even email was new, exotic, and expensive back then.

The real breakthrough came with the user-friendly access made possible by the World Wide Web. As a young student, Marc Andreessen, now one of the most successful startup investors, was among the principal developers of the first web browser—initially Mosaic, later Netscape. The

company Netscape became one of the early internet icons, thanks to its spectacular IPO in August 1995, just one year after its founding, and also because of the ensuing browser wars with Microsoft and its eventual acquisition by AOL.

Netscape transformed the internet into the World Wide Web and made it accessible to the general public through its ease of use. That simple, global access laid the foundation for the spectacular boom and for the major corporations that followed—Amazon, Google, Facebook, Microsoft, eBay, and Uber, among many others.

Decentralized access promised democratization. No longer could a handful of media conglomerates be the gatekeepers who decided what news should reach us; now, anyone had the power to publish. Borders in commerce were expected to vanish. And the smartphone, permanently connected to the internet, would combine many functions in one device: calendar, alarm clock, maps, dating, wallet, investment advisor, fitness coach and nutritionist, exam preparation, movies, and much, much more. Our entire lives have been absorbed by smartphones. Without it, we're helpless. We suffer from withdrawal, and lose touch with our friends. It is no surprise that Apple, whose iPhone holds only about a 20% market share but generates substantial profits for the company, ended 2024 as the most valuable company in the world with a market capitalization of around $3.5 trillion. Without the internet, there would be no iPhone, or at least it would be a much more boring one.

In principle, the internet is open and accessible to everyone. It is a platform on which countless other platforms have been built, and an ecosystem that has permeated every corner of society, the economy, and personal life. Above all, it's a network that becomes ever more valuable the more it is used.

In the mid-1990s, when Amazon was only one year old, and Google had not yet been founded, skepticism still prevailed. The internet was cumbersome to use; websites were often unreachable or difficult to find; building them was difficult; and it seemed like it might be something only interesting to geeks—certainly not for the mass market. The first signs of commercialization were met with fierce criticism. Who would want to give up the experience of browsing for books in a bookstore with the personalized advice and the atmosphere? No, online shopping would surely never catch on.

What does this have to do with Bitcoin?

The parallels are striking. The technological architecture is quite similar. The following figure illustrates this.

FIGURE 7 (p. 133): Bitcoin is the Internet of Value

The internet revolutionized the storage, transmission, and access to information, and bitcoin is revolutionizing the storage, transmission, and access to value. It is now just as easy to send bitcoin over the Bitcoin network as it is to send an email or a text message around the globe. Even within Germany's own borders, a simple bank transfer can take three days, and it takes even longer if it falls on a weekend. If you want to send money to Canada, Africa, or South America, it could take more than a week for the recipient

Bitcoin Is the Internet of Value

Comparison of the Internet and Bitcoin

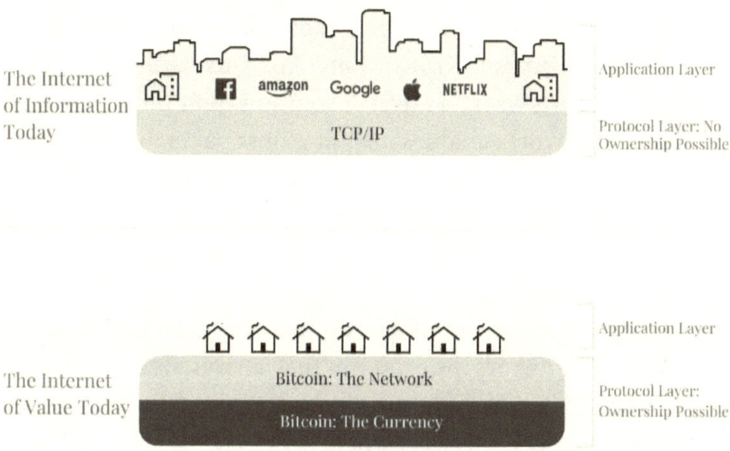

Source: Croesus_BTC (X)

to receive your payment. On top of that, there are often significant fees and the risk that an intermediary bank may reject the transaction or block access to your account along the way. But as long as you have an internet connection, access to the Bitcoin network cannot be blocked.

And just as massive platforms have been built on the internet, similar platforms can be built over the Bitcoin network. The first ones are already emerging—exchanges such as Coinbase, Kraken, and Austria's Bitpanda. The Lightning Network, a Layer-2 solution built on top of the Bitcoin network, enables instant global payments at near-zero cost. Jack Mallers has built a very successful company, Strike, on this foundation. Microsoft is developing an identity solution, ION (Identity Overlay Network), built on the Bitcoin network.

The criticism that the fledgling internet faced in the mid-1990s mirrors the criticism that surrounds the Bitcoin network today: *Hard to use, underdeveloped—why do you really need it?—there are other ways; it's mainly used for illegal purposes.*

Criticism is easy. It is more difficult to have the imagination and the ability to implement new applications. What is now possible that wasn't possible before, or could only previously be done with great difficulty or effort? What second- or third-order effects might arise—innovations that build upon prior innovations? The internet enabled Facebook. Facebook made highly personalized advertising possible. The smartphone made advertising mobile and localized. The next step is for us to enter into virtual worlds. Who could have foreseen that in the mid-1990s?

The same is true for the Bitcoin network. Value can be transferred globally both very quickly (in ten minutes via the Bitcoin network; instantly via Lightning) and inexpensively, without slow, bureaucratic intermediaries, and without the risk of failure. At first glance, this simply improves an existing process (money transfers). But at second glance, it could mean that the approximately two billion people worldwide who currently lack access to the financial system might finally be able to participate, provided they have an internet connection and a smartphone. That not only translates into far better participation in economic life for these individuals but also into more consumers, higher living standards, greater innovation, and a more competitive global marketplace. Through the Lightning Network, which enables small payments over the Bitcoin network, micropayments in the sub-cent range can be made globally, instantly, and at virtually no cost. With Lightning, a consumer in Central America could shop online, top up the prepaid card, and pay, and all without needing to go near a bank account or credit card.

The Bitcoin network will also give rise to new financial products. Traditional financial products can be tokenized and thus made easily accessible online. Larry Fink, CEO of the world's largest asset manager, BlackRock, said that "tokenization is the next generation for markets" and spoke of the *tokenization of everything*. Tokenization means, for example, that a bond is not booked into a securities account at a bank but held directly in your own wallet.

The virtual universes created by the internet are vast. But ultimately, they revolve around information. The universes that will be created via blockchain technologies, especially the Bitcoin network, will be even bigger. And this time, it won't just be about information; it will be about monetary value.

Both the internet and Bitcoin are protocols and networks on which applications are built. The main difference is that bitcoin's fixed supply functions as the currency of the Bitcoin network and reflects its value. Anyone can participate in it financially simply by buying bitcoin. With the internet, by contrast, you can only financially participate in its value appreciation by investing in companies on the application layer, such as Facebook, Amazon, or Google—and for most people, that's only possible after they've gone public, which often happens quite late, after many years of successful development.

Bitcoin is different. You can participate in the development of its network at any time with nothing more than a smartphone and a Bitcoin wallet. You don't even need a bank account or a brokerage account. Nowadays, there are financial products such as ETFs and ETNs that are backed by bitcoin and track its value 1:1. You can simply buy these as securities through a traditional brokerage account at your bank. ETNs (exchange-traded notes) are technically unsecured debt securities, but they are usually fully collateralized with bitcoin and issued by a bank or financial institution, although they do not grant you direct ownership of the underlying assets.

Just as the value of the internet and companies based on it has fluctuated over time, the same has been true for the value development of the Bitcoin network. Nevertheless, Bitcoin is actually less risky because there is no company behind it, no management team, and, in principle, no employees—it is an autonomous system run by many independent participants and controlled by no one. Unlike with companies, there's no counterparty risk, no board of directors making good or bad business decisions. You don't have to analyze companies, markets, competitors, business models, or management teams. Bitcoin is therefore less complex than individual companies or industries. Once you understand it, little changes. To participate in the Internet of Value, all you need to do is buy bitcoin.

Section 5:
Challenges and Criticisms

Chapter 16:
March 12, 2020

The signs had been brewing for a few weeks. In China, the entrances to apartment buildings were being welded shut. In Italy, intensive care beds were suddenly at capacity. In the U.S., a great many people in nursing homes were suddenly dying. The COVID-19 pandemic was threatening to become a massive global crisis. That it was highly contagious was obvious, but whether it was as dangerous as it really remained unclear. People prepared themselves for lockdowns, remote work, and a full-blown crisis, turning to panic buying and emergency planning. Everyone grew nervous, and the financial markets even more so.

It caught up with me on March 12, 2020. A colleague of mine, who had participated in a team meeting the day before with many others, had tested positive. This was occurring throughout Germany, indeed throughout Europe. Maximum uncertainty sent the financial markets into near collapse that day. How significant would the damage be to society and the economy? How high would the death toll rise? Would the economy, entire societies, even the world and humanity with it, come to an end? Investors fled to supposedly safe, liquid assets. Everything was sold off.

On March 12, 2020, bitcoin fell by over 50%.

At our company, we initiated the third stage of our emergency plan. Everyone was sent home, and the office was cleared out. On the way home, I had a sinking feeling. The startup portfolio we had built up over fifteen years would collapse, and the financial markets would be beaten down for good. Furthermore, bitcoin was not the stable asset we had hoped for after all. The price fell relentlessly all day, at one point by more than 50%.

In the spur of the moment, I ended my annual three-month alcohol-free stretch, drove to the supermarket, and bought a bottle of whiskey.

As the evening wore on, the whiskey could hardly dull the bad feeling I was harboring, caused by bitcoin's continued decline. What turned things around was my wife's remark that we should have sold near the all-time high at the end of 2017, just as she'd advised. I heard the word *sell* and immediately thought *buy*. The entire crash was triggered by fear, which was certainly partly justified but also highly emotional and overblown. It was pure panic.

Shortly after midnight, and now no longer sober, I bought more bitcoin—one of the best decisions I ever made, as the price would quadruple by year's end and increase 25-fold by the end of 2024.

The extreme fluctuations in bitcoin's price obscure the reality that the Bitcoin network, the technology itself, is extremely stable, hardly changes, and is highly predictable.

Chapter 16

Bitcoin's software undergoes major updates only every few years, implemented only after a lengthy and complex process and with widespread acceptance. The software is open source, meaning it is accessible to anyone. For over seventeen years, it has behaved as intended. A new block is created every ten minutes on average, and its size, therefore, the number of transactions it can contain, is fixed. Also completely unchanged is the fact that the maximum number of bitcoin to ever be created—21 million—will be reached in the year 2140.

Chapter 17:
Bitcoin Cycles: Bitcoin Crashes All The Time

The volatility of bitcoin is one of the main reasons why many people stay away from it, or fail to understand it. How can something be considered a superior store of value if its price fluctuates so wildly? On any given day, swings of 10% up or down are entirely possible. And sometimes significantly more, as we saw on March 12, 2020, when the price was cut in half. Over longer periods, fluctuations can be even greater. In 2022, bitcoin lost about 65% of its value as measured in euros. Compared to other asset classes, bitcoin was the worst performer in 2022, but the best in 2021, 2023, and 2024. Large price fluctuations create stress. Losses, even if unrealized, can feel heavier emotionally than equally sized gains. People are generally risk-averse, often preferring to avoid losses even if it means forgoing higher gains.

Bitcoin has consistently exhibited higher volatility than almost any other asset class. There are several reasons for this. Unlike stocks, for example, bitcoin is traded worldwide around the clock. Market phases with low liquidity recur, during which large buy or sell orders can trigger strong price movements. Much of the trading occurs on unregulated exchanges, and, as a relatively young asset class, bitcoin attracts day traders and short-term speculators. Many Bitcoiners, by contrast, hold their coins for the long term, refusing to sell regardless of short- or medium-term price fluctuations. On top of that, an estimated two to four million bitcoin have been *lost*. Their owners have lost access to them. Experts estimate that only around six to eight million bitcoin are realistically available for purchase. As of October 2024, around 2.3 million bitcoin sit on exchanges, meaning they are readily available in the short term. While this amount corresponded to a substantial market value of $140 billion at that time, periods of low liquidity suggest that significant buy or sell orders can still move the market.

In addition to short-term fluctuations, bitcoin has experienced four distinct periods since 2011 in which the price declined by more than 70% from an all-time high (ATH), resulting in prolonged bear markets.

> Figure 8 (p. 147): The price of bitcoin (black line) and drawdowns from the all-time high over time (dark gray line).

The chart shows the price of bitcoin in black on a logarithmic scale (right axis) and the percentage drawdowns from each all-time high in dark gray (left axis). Since 2011, four major cycles have been identified, with drawdowns

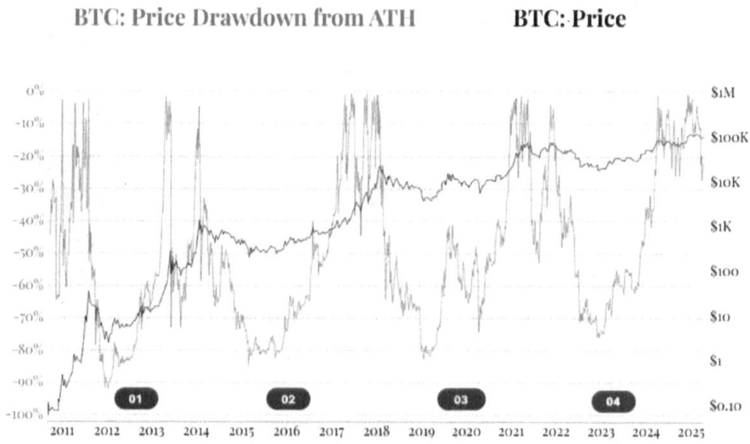

Source: Authors' illustration and Glassnode

exceeding 70%, the first exceeding 90%. Interesting patterns can be found, especially across the three most recent bear markets (2, 3, and 4). It is worth noting that during the first bear market, Bitcoin was still very young and *immature*, so its significance is limited.

What stands out in these patterns? First, each cycle begins by reaching a new all-time high (ATH). The drawdowns, declines from the ATH, that follow are dramatic, ranging from 70% to 90%. Yet the cycles run in a remarkably parallel way: they last approximately four years. After reaching a previous all-time high, bitcoin goes on to set new, higher highs. There are several points at which the drawdown approaches the zero line, each marking a new, higher all-time high.

The regularity of the cycles is remarkable. In the last three bear markets, it took about a year (twelve to fourteen months) to get from the ATH to the cycle's low point. It took almost exactly two more years to reach the previous ATH in bear markets 2 and 3. In the current cycle (4), the old ATH was reached slightly more quickly, after about a year and a half.

The interval between regaining a previous ATH and reaching the next can be relatively short. Prices often increase rapidly and steeply. In the last two bear markets, a new ATH was reached within approximately twelve months of regaining the previous ATH. Taken together, the entire recent cycle has roughly corresponded to bitcoin's four-year halving period. The chart shows that the current cycle, number 4, is likely not yet over as of October 2024. The previous ATH of November 2021 was reached again and only slightly surpassed in March 2024. If the fourth cycle follows a pattern similar to the previous ones, the next significantly higher ATH may not occur until late 2025.

In each case, each new ATH has been well above the previous one. Rising demand is met by an issuance schedule that halves the supply of bitcoin every four years, driving prices higher as adoption and demand increase.

The sometimes sharp short-term volatility (and the cyclical, prolonged twelve-month declines of more than 70% from ATHs) can obscure bitcoin's core—a store of value and therefore a protection against inflation, not in the short term but in the medium and especially the long term. Measured against fiat currencies, bitcoin's value may not be preserved in the short run, even for as long as three years after an all-time high. But over longer horizons of at least four years, history so far (seventeen years and counting) has shown otherwise. For this reason, the time horizon for an investment should be at least four years. At present, bitcoin is not yet suitable as a short-term investment.

At bitcoin's core is the immutable, limited cap of 21 million coins. As it is more widely accepted and demand increases, its price rises. In contrast, at the core of traditional fiat currencies lies an ever-expanding money supply in a debt-based system driven by perpetual debt issuance by governments, corporations, and consumers. Globally, the money supply grows almost continuously, with only brief interruptions, whereas the growth of real GNP is much slower. Considering the growing supply of fiat money, it's obvious that bitcoin will become more *valuable* over time.

The following chart shows the development of the M2 money supply in the U.S. It briefly declined after 2021 due to the interest rate hike cycle, but by October 2024, it was climbing again to record highs.[26]

FIGURE 9 (p. 151): Development of the U.S. money supply, M2, since 1960

The same pattern can be found in other asset classes—gold, stocks, and, in some cases, real estate—all tend to rise over the long term at roughly the same pace as growth in the money supply. In ancient Rome, a fine toga (the equivalent of a modern-day suit) cost roughly an ounce of gold. Today, a fancy custom-made suit still costs about the same—an ounce of gold. In real terms, as measured by the price of suits, gold has at least preserved its value, and may have appreciated slightly. In a presentation that's well worth seeing, Michael Saylor vividly illustrates, among other things, the parallel between money supply growth and the S&P 500. Over the long term, stocks hardly seem to outperform monetary expansion. This means that it is at least partly the money supply, rather than the real value growth of companies, that drives stock prices.[27]

FIGURE 10 (p. 152): Development of M2 money supply and stock prices over time

Conversely, this also means that any asset growing slower than the money supply represents a real loss of value.

The M2 Money Supply Has Grown Almost Continuously since 1960

Development of the M2 money supply in the U.S.

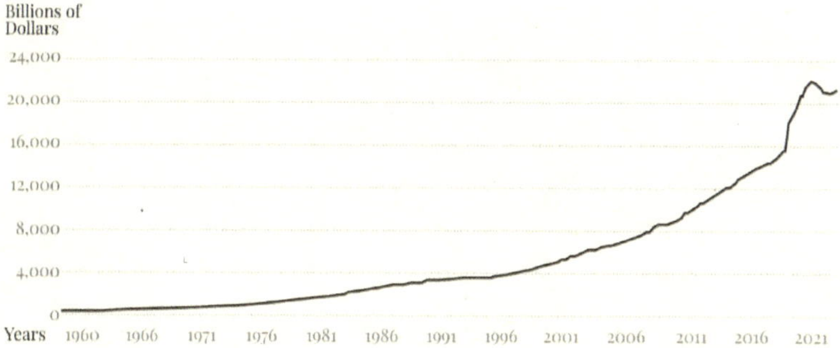

Source: Board of Governors of the Federal Reserve System; Federal Reserve Bank of St. Louis.

Stock Market Growth Is Largely Driven by Monetary Expansion

Comparison of the Development of M2 and the S&P 500 Index

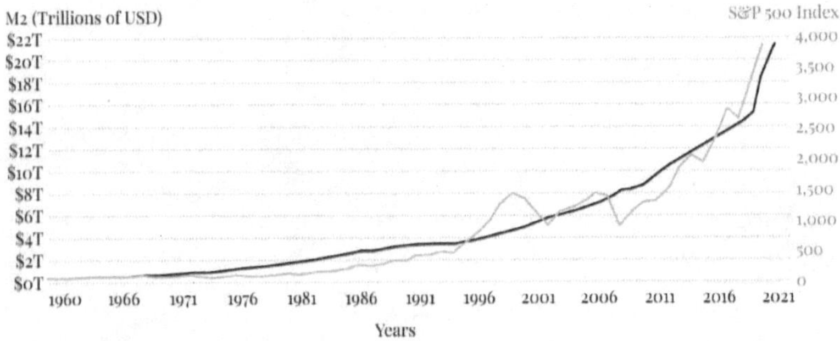

Source: Strategy[8]

Bitcoin adoption and use are still in a very early phase. Very few individuals own it, and hardly any companies have purchased it. Only since the approval of U.S. ETFs in January 2024 have many institutional investors been able to acquire bitcoin. Only a few countries (such as Bhutan and El Salvador) have added bitcoin to their reserves. It's suspected that other countries, similar to Bhutan, may be acquiring bitcoin through their own mining activities, possibly including some of the Arab nations or Russia. Other countries, such as China and the United States, have seized bitcoin linked to illegal activities, though it remains unclear whether they intend to retain these coins permanently. The real opportunity lies in the increasing adoption of bitcoin, which could lead to a value appreciation far exceeding the rate of money supply growth. Since 2020, even with the steep drawdown of 2022, bitcoin has risen by an average of nearly 50% per year. Even if these returns taper off in the future, they will likely remain well ahead of those of other asset classes on average. Bitcoin is expected to remain one of the most attractive investments for many years, perhaps decades, to come.

The short-term fluctuations are just like a fog that clouds our view, making it difficult to see Bitcoin for what it truly is. You have to look through the fog to clearly see the core. It is both human and entirely understandable for price fluctuations to cause stress. *I would rather deal with 10% inflation than the 65% drawdown of 2022.* Viewed through the lens of all-time highs alone, bitcoin does not appear to function well as a store of value if the price remains significantly below that high for more than three years.

How do you deal with these fluctuations?

"When in doubt, zoom out," they say in the Bitcoin community. Adopt a longer-term perspective, and you will see that bitcoin functions not only as a store of value but also as a highly profitable investment. Continuously buying, for example by dollar-cost averaging, through a downturn, as we have seen in Chapter 12, increases the return on bitcoin.

When you consider Bitcoin's fundamental properties, especially the lack of central control and its resistance to dilution in contrast to a constantly diluting financial system, its superiority quickly becomes clear. Bitcoin is what it is. It does not change. Transactions are added to new blocks on the blockchain at predictable ten-minute intervals. The underlying software doesn't change substantially. Relevant updates only occur every few years, such as SegWit in 2017 or Taproot in 2021.

SegWit, short for *Segregated Witness*, refers to a Bitcoin protocol update that was implemented in 2017. It was developed to address some of Bitcoin's technical limitations, particularly scalability. Taproot was another Bitcoin protocol upgrade, activated in November 2021, that improved privacy, efficiency, and flexibility for bitcoin transactions.

Meanwhile, in the negative sense, the financial system doesn't change either. It continues to dilute itself rather than learn from its mistakes. Government budgets are not repaired; rather, they deteriorate. They become increasingly unsound as interest rates rise and debt burdens balloon. The interest burden from U.S. federal debt rose from $1 billion per day in 2019 to $2 billion per day in 2022 and to $3 billion per day—over $1 trillion per year—by 2024 or 2025.

That said, it must be acknowledged that bitcoin's price declines can be severe, and it can take time for losses to be recouped. This can lead to considerable stress. You might develop a feeling of unease, or struggle to sleep, or—worst of all—panic sell all your bitcoin in an impulsive, emotional reaction. Yet so far, there has never been a four-year period in which bitcoin ended up lower than it was before, even if you had bought some at an all-time high. Historically, bitcoin's price gains have always far outweighed its corrections. With every crash, bitcoin appears to have emerged stronger. Ultimately, it is conviction, patience, and emotional stability that pay off.

Chapter 18:
Bitcoin: Rough Edges and Negative Perceptions

Bitcoin is not an easy concept to grasp. For the vast majority of people, it does not make intuitive sense and takes several attempts to understand how it works. And almost everyone needs one or even a few friends to help them make sense of it. The issue is that most people get stuck on one-sided criticisms and never get to the heart of the matter.

Bitcoin May Be Limited, but There Is an Unlimited Number of Cryptocurrencies

This superficial argument prevented me from examining Bitcoin more closely in 2013. I lumped all the different blockchain technologies together and failed to see the difference—that Bitcoin is the only truly decentralized solution. The seemingly unlimited number of possible crypto technologies obscured the fact that only bitcoin is truly and immutably limited with its cap of 21 million.

A Medium for Illicit Transactions

Bitcoin is seen as the shady currency of criminals on the internet, used for money laundering, drug trafficking, and other illicit activities. However, there have always been illegal activities, and various payment systems have been used to facilitate them: cash, gold, diamonds, shell companies, art, real estate, and so on. Bitcoin is only particularly well-suited for this at first glance because its peer-to-peer transactions occur outside the existing financial system, with no intermediaries, especially government intermediaries.

However, Bitcoin is not completely anonymous. Transactions on the blockchain are transparent and stored forever. Once a single Bitcoin address can be tied to a real identity, it's easy to link every other transaction from this address to that identity. It takes a great deal of effort to truly anonymize a bitcoin transaction. Even minor errors can compromise the pseudonymity of the Bitcoin blockchain and expose the owner. Repeatedly, law enforcement agencies have identified the individuals behind illicit transactions on the Bitcoin blockchain.

A common mistake is when a person sends illegally acquired bitcoin to an exchange account and identifies themselves to exchange it for fiat currency. Once an anonymous Bitcoin address is linked to a non-anonymous one, the anonymity of that address is lost forever. Various sources estimate that the share of illegal transactions conducted with bitcoin is lower than that conducted with fiat currencies. According to Chainalysis's "Crypto Crime Report 2024," only 0.34% of bitcoin transactions have been linked to illegal activity.[28]

Price Volatility

As discussed in the last chapter, bitcoin fluctuates more than almost all other major asset classes, including stocks, real estate, bonds, gold, and oil. Given its large fluctuations and a short-term investment horizon, bitcoin may appear anything but a store of value: unattractive at best and emotionally exhausting at worst. After all, who enjoys opening their portfolio to see a loss of 60% on paper? The vast majority of investors, at least in Germany, are so risk-averse that they'd rather put their money into a savings account that shows no downward value fluctuations but also generates practically no return. In real terms, after factoring in the loss of purchasing power due to inflation, money in a savings account inevitably loses value, slowly but surely. For those who would rather forgo returns to avoid nominal losses in value, bitcoin will always appear to be a difficult investment.

It's only with a longer timeframe—one measured in years—that bitcoin reveals its high positive returns in fiat terms. Over the same period, fiat currencies steadily lose substantial value due to inflation. That's the key—a long-term perspective versus short-term thinking. This is why those with a lower time preference, who care less about short-term consumption and more about the future, tend to adopt Bitcoin sooner than those living mainly in the here and now.

Bitcoin Can Be Hacked or Stolen

Time and again we hear about hacks where bitcoin has been stolen. In 2014, Mt. Gox, the largest Bitcoin exchange at the time, filed for bankruptcy and halted all withdrawals after it was revealed that 650,000 bitcoin had been lost or stolen. The theft of coins stored on exchanges has happened countless times since then. However, the attack targeted not the Bitcoin blockchain itself but exchange-operated software. It is also often unclear whether these involved external theft or were instead a form of embezzlement committed by the exchange operators themselves. After all, they have full access to the bitcoin stored there. The temptation is obvious because bitcoin will never all be withdrawn at the same time. As banks do, one could use customers' assets for lending or for supposedly better investments.

Some bitcoin holders have lost their coins due to loss of access to their private keys. Sometimes the keys were genuinely lost; other times they were stolen; for example, if stored unencrypted in a cloud account or written on a piece of paper at home.

The important point is that neither bitcoin nor the blockchain itself—the actual technology—has ever been hacked. Aside from a few software bugs early on, the system has always worked exactly as intended. The software is open and transparent. Once a transaction is recorded on the blockchain, it cannot be altered. A payment made to a specific recipient some time ago cannot later be redirected to someone else, nor can it be reversed. There is no central authority that could *correct* a supposed wrong or mistaken transaction. No one can punish a bitcoin holder for misconduct by confiscating their coins.

Regulation and Government Bans

Even before the SEC approved bitcoin ETFs, its then-chair, Gary Gensler, spoke very positively about Bitcoin from a regulatory perspective: "Everything other than Bitcoin is a security; only Bitcoin is true money."[29]

In the beginning, bitcoin was largely unregulated. Gradually, however, a patchwork of global regulations has emerged, ranging from outright governmental bans to El Salvador's recognition of bitcoin as legal tender. It is true that if all countries in the world coordinated to ban bitcoin and imposed draconian penalties for owning it, its further adoption would at least be severely curtailed. Perhaps Bitcoin would then be reduced to a marginal niche or disappear altogether. However, the probability of such global coordination is zero. Rather, such a scenario would create strong incentives for some countries to gain advantages over others by creating more favorable regulations. Even within the European Union, tax laws are highly fragmented, as member states either simply cannot or will not coordinate, or at times deliberately seek competitive advantages over each other. As long as there are benefits to be gained from using Bitcoin, there will be legal pathways to enable its use.

Electricity Consumption: *Bitcoin is Killing the Planet*

Yes, Bitcoin does consume substantial energy. That is not a bug, but a feature of it. Behind the electricity consumption lies the massive computing power of the Bitcoin miners. This computing power, known as hashrate, serves as a protective wall that prevents malicious actors with greater computing power from rewriting the blockchain with *fraudulent* transactions or altering existing ones. The computing power of miners requires electricity.

Electricity consumption in itself is harmless; what matters is how the electricity is generated. The burning of fossil fuels for power generation releases CO_2 that has been sequestered for millions of years, a major contributor to global warming. There have been various attempts to determine the energy mix of Bitcoin miners. A variety of statistics indicate that the majority now comes from renewable energy sources.[30]

In particular, the use of *excess* renewable energy—energy that would otherwise go unused—for Bitcoin mining is in no way harmful to the environment. Again and again, there's a mismatch between the renewable energy that could be generated and the ability to transport it to consumers, or even to find buyers at all. In Germany, this leads to wind turbines being shut down on windy days. In 2021 alone, the Federal Network Agency reported over €800 million in compensation payments to energy producers for electricity that went unused. Provided Bitcoin mining is profitable, the returns miners could generate from using that surplus power would far exceed this amount.[31]

Bitcoin also promotes the expansion of renewable energy because, in addition to regular electricity consumption, Bitcoin mining can ensure plants operate at full capacity. A guaranteed buyer for 100% of the electricity generated significantly increases the probability that a wind power plant will be profitable. Thus, Bitcoin mining creates a direct, unsubsidized incentive to expand renewable energy sources.

Moreover, Bitcoin can help stabilize the power grid. During the winter of 2022–2023 in Texas, when power generation decreased while demand increased, Bitcoin miners were quickly shut down. Unlike industrial processes, Bitcoin miners can pause operations on short notice without damaging equipment, thereby reducing electricity demand and stabilizing the grid. By shutting down flexibly, Bitcoin miners can complement other consumers, such as AI data centers that cannot be easily turned off, thereby adding flexibility to the overall system. Ultimately, coupling mining with renewable generation creates a minimum price for electricity at which it can always be sold. This guarantees plant utilization and, consequently, its profitability, which in turn drives further expansion of renewable energy.

Slow Evolution of Bitcoin Core Technology

Changes to the Bitcoin software are made only through elaborate coordination and testing processes. Major upgrades included the introduction of SegWit in 2017 and Taproot in 2021. The slow and deliberate evolution protects the Bitcoin technology from flawed developments and bugs. Users, and indeed the entire ecosystem, can be sure that Bitcoin will continue to function just as well in the future as it does today. No malicious or incompetent central authority can impose changes for its own benefit at the expense of everyone else.

Relevant developments typically do not occur within the Bitcoin software itself but rather in applications or protocols that build on top of the blockchain, i.e., Layer-2 solutions. The Lightning Network, for example, built on the Bitcoin network, is capable of processing very fast and virtually free global payments, unlike Bitcoin's main chain. The disadvantage of making transactions on the Bitcoin blockchain, which require at least ten minutes to be finalized, is offset by the Lightning Network. In this sense, Bitcoin is both structurally conservative and highly innovative: the so-called main layer changes only rarely and minimally, while additional layers connected to it can flexibly and innovatively expand Bitcoin's capabilities.

Acceptance Is Still Low

You can't pay with bitcoin; nobody accepts it. This is both true and not true. True on the one hand, because Bitcoin has yet to reach the mainstream. Restaurants or shops that accept it remain the exception, although a variety of websites provide directories of places that do. But there are major variations in acceptance around the globe: in El Salvador, where bitcoin is effectively legal tender, many businesses do accept it, and the number of those that do is growing. The same applies to the Swiss city of Lugano and to countries with high inflation, such as Turkey, Argentina, and several African countries.[32]

Indirect acceptance is also possible via Visa or Mastercard credit cards linked to a Bitcoin wallet. Coinbase, Bitwala, or Swissquote, for example, offer such cards. When you pay with them, the euro or dollar amount is converted into bitcoin at the current exchange rate plus a small fee, then the corresponding amount of bitcoin is withdrawn from your linked wallet. This means you can pay with bitcoin worldwide indirectly via the Visa and Mastercard networks.

Decentralization Means No One Can Help You

The Bitcoin network has no central authority. The blockchain is distributed across tens of thousands of nodes, such that copies of it exist everywhere. New blocks are added through competition among miners distributed worldwide. No one has central control or can unilaterally change anything. This also means that a payment sent to an incorrect address by mistake can only be reversed by the recipient, not by anyone else. In principle, bitcoin sent to the wrong address are lost.

Access to bitcoin is managed through a *wallet*. There are two types: non-custodial wallets and custodial wallets. With a non-custodial wallet, only you have access to and control over your bitcoin. The wallet holds the private key that enables access to the blockchain. If you lose access to the wallet or your private key, no one can recover it for you; you alone are responsible for it. There is no central authority that can restore a lost password or private key. The upside to this is that absolutely no one, but you, has access to your bitcoin. A custodial wallet, by contrast, is managed by a third party who controls the actual access to your bitcoin. As with a bank account, you yourself have password-protected access. If you lose or forget your password, the custodian can reset it. The downside here is that the custodian, or someone instructing them, can also deny your access to your bitcoin.

Non-Inflationary Money Leads to Deflation and a Collapse of the Economy

This argument has merit; in a highly indebted system, deflation can indeed trigger collapse. Ultimately, in a deflationary environment, debt grows in real terms, and economic activity slows in anticipation of falling prices. Unemployment and business bankruptcies can follow. It is argued that this could create a deflationary spiral: unemployment leads to lower demand, which in turn leads to company bankruptcies, which further lowers demand, and so forth.

But deflation is not inherently destructive. The very strong economic growth of the 19th century under the full gold standard proves this, as do deflationary trends in modern sectors such as the computer and electronics industries. Despite the expectation that computers and smartphones will get increasingly better and cheaper, people still buy them. Far from collapsing, these industries have thrived. Rapid technological progress has not only led to falling prices but also to many more effective products. In fact, this should be the case across practically all industries. Technological progress and productivity gains should, generally speaking, translate into lower prices. Inflation robs us of purchasing power in two ways: directly through price increases, and indirectly by preventing consumers from benefiting from productivity gains unless wages rise in real terms. This is at least the case for the lower-income classes. In a deflationary environment, by contrast, productivity gains could flow directly to consumers via falling prices.

Section 6:
Effects

Chapter 19:
You Don't Change Bitcoin; Bitcoin Changes You

A well-known saying in the Bitcoin community is "You don't change Bitcoin. Bitcoin changes you." The first part establishes that no central authority can alter Bitcoin's fundamental properties. Since January 3, 2009, Bitcoin's function has been essentially unchanged. Only bug fixes, minor tweaks, and a few more significant updates have been made following a rigorous review process. The exciting question now is how Bitcoin changes us—as individuals, as businesses, as a society, or even as nations?

Modesty and a Focus on Quality

In April 2021, I conducted an experiment where I paid for all my purchases, at least as many as possible, with bitcoin. In Germany, this is only possible indirectly. With the exception of a few events and some online shops, there are still very few businesses that accept bitcoin directly.

But indirectly, it works through various credit cards that convert the euro amount at checkout into bitcoin at the current exchange rate, deducting it from a linked Bitcoin wallet. Coinbase, Bitwala, and the Swiss bank Swissquote, for example, offer such cards. You can either buy bitcoin through their exchanges or deposit bitcoin directly into the wallet they manage. Using the Visa credit card function, these bitcoin can then be spent anywhere that Visa is accepted, so virtually anywhere in the world, and since the pandemic, almost everywhere in Germany as well. The only drawback is that this is a so-called custodial wallet. That means you don't hold the private key to the wallet yourself but must trust the provider to ensure that the bitcoin you've deposited are really there.

So I used my Visa card to pay for all my expenses, which meant that I was indirectly paying with bitcoin.

What effects did I observe?

First, I spent less. I found it much harder to part with bitcoin than with euros. Even though it's the same mathematically, bitcoin felt more valuable. I expected excellent long-term appreciation and preferred to hold onto them. Of course, one could just as well spend fewer euros and use the savings to buy bitcoin, but this would involve many more steps and a lot of extra effort. All of this becomes clear through the famous *Bitcoin pizza* example. On May 22, 2010, Laszlo Hanyecz paid 10,000 bitcoin for two pizzas, which at the time were worth $20. By January 2025, those same 10,000 bitcoin would equal around $1 billion. Those two pizzas are often referred to as the most expensive in history. Yet basically anyone who spent $20 on anything on May 22, 2010, could have also bought 10,000 bitcoin with it. The difference lies in whether you spend the bitcoin directly, or spend a fiat currency that could have been used to buy bitcoin. People are reluctant to part with good money; the loss has more of a sting, even if, in the moment, it makes no difference whether they are spending bitcoin or euros.

I bought fewer rolls at the bakery; on some Sundays, we ate cereal or regular bread instead. On business trips, I skipped the occasional coffee or beer and ate more modestly. Staunch Keynesians see this behavior as the beginning of the end of the economic system. To them, a lack of demand signals the onset of the deflationary death spiral: once the economy stops growing, prices fall, making it more attractive to delay purchases, which in turn reduces demand further. One company after another goes bankrupt, unemployment soars, and the economy and society collapse.

I won't dig deeper into Keynesian demand theory here, except to say that consuming less useless stuff is better for the planet due to reduced resource consumption, for our own health, and for society as a whole. Lower consumption also means greater savings—savings that reduce individuals' dependence on state welfare systems, strengthen society's collective support systems, and generate funds for investment.

The second effect was even more surprising: I bought higher-quality and therefore more expensive things. If I were going to part with my bitcoin, I wanted to get something worthwhile in return. I'd choose the slightly more expensive wine over the cheap one, enjoy it all the more, and drink wine much less often overall. The result was both more enjoyment and more savings. A few years ago, I bought a new refrigerator. The old one was about twenty years old, still working fine, but it used too much electricity. It now serves as a backup and party fridge in the basement. I was surprised when the salesperson explained that the new refrigerator, a high-quality German brand-name product, would likely last only eight to ten years. That's just how it is these days. But shouldn't technological progress mean that things last longer? Clearly, the fiat system incentivizes not only short-term consumption but also ever-declining quality. In a depreciating fiat system with inflating money, the incentive shifts toward making cheap purchases and low-cost consumption, and consequently toward cheaper production and poorer quality. In my own purchasing behavior, I observed that bitcoin encourages the opposite: if you have to part with your bitcoin, you'd rather buy something of high quality.

The third effect, however, was the most surprising of all. I actually had more bitcoin at the end of the experiment than at the beginning. Each time I reluctantly parted with a few satoshis, I was overcome with the urge to buy even more. Rounding up generously on these purchases resulted in a larger bitcoin balance than at the start of the experiment. Good money that holds its value over time is simply more attractive than money that is inflated.

Longer-Term Thinking or Lower Time Preference

If I know my money will be worthless tomorrow, I have to spend it today. But if I believe my money will be worth more tomorrow, then I have an incentive to wait—to live more modestly, to save, and perhaps to do without a thing or two. My preference for short-term consumption goes down. I don't need everything today; it can wait until tomorrow or even the day after. What naturally follows is the tendency to think more long-term.

The famous psychology experiment, the Marshmallow Test, is a strong predictor of a child's future success. In the test, a child is given a tasty marshmallow with the promise of a second one if they don't eat the first right away. Many children find it difficult to resist for even a short period, such as fifteen minutes. Although the return of 100% after those fifteen minutes is substantial, many cannot manage it. Short-term sacrifice is almost always a central prerequisite for long-term success. Any investment requires foregoing consumption in the short term. A five-year degree, for example, means giving up income and leisure now in exchange for the vague hope of a better job and higher income later on. Athletic success requires training. Strong personal relationships and friendships come only after investing time and commitment.

The more you start to think long-term, the more long-term personal questions arise. How do I want to grow old? How, where, and above all, with whom do I want to spend that time? What do I want to have done by then? What do I want to leave behind? Lots of money? A little money? A meaningful contribution to society? What must I do today, tomorrow, and the next day to achieve the long-term goals I want to be remembered for?

It permeates absolutely all areas of life. If you want to be healthy in old age, you need to start thinking about diet and exercise now. What good is a lot of money if you're unhealthy or lonely? Personal relationships, too, take on a new meaning when seen from a long-term perspective. A low time preference creates a much greater willingness to invest in relationships and to be genuinely interested in others. The incentive to exploit others for personal gain shrinks dramatically or disappears altogether.

Many Bitcoiners talk about their friendship circles changing. People with a short-term perspective who act at the expense of others simply fit less into the worldview and self-image of these Bitcoiners. Their paths diverge.

When you operate from a long-term perspective, time itself feels more abundant, and so you become far more willing to invest it: in others, in yourself, in society. You're more open to new things, more optimistic. The future looks bright. In the fiat system, the future strips away your purchasing power—and with it, your lifetime—through inflation. Living by a Bitcoin standard, the future opens up opportunities. The future feels positive.

Bitcoin Strengthens Personal Responsibility

Without inflation and with a lower time preference—that is, with a low preference for the present—saving is optimal. A long-term perspective makes you aware that emergencies can happen. You become increasingly attuned to your own and others' future needs, particularly in old age. You both can and want to provide for yourself. Savings and strong relationships are associated with a long-term outlook and reduce dependence on government support. Anyone who holds bitcoin in their own wallet is taking responsibility for themselves, and, to some extent, they gain independence from third parties. The ability and willingness to do so spills over into other areas of life. First and foremost, you're responsible for yourself, and only in an emergency does your community step in. Given demographic trends, state pensions will provide little more than minimal, last-resort coverage of your future needs. Although this has been openly discussed for decades, you only truly begin to understand it once you've adopted a long-term perspective and a fundamental sense of your own personal responsibility.

Bitcoin Sharpens Critical Thinking

The fiat money system is dishonest. Money is supposed to remain stable, yet stability is equated with a 2% currency devaluation. At 2% depreciation, the value of money is halved in the *long run*, i.e., within about thirty-five years. That is not stable. Debts are labeled as assets, as with the so-called special funds for climate protection and the armed forces. But they are not assets; they're debts. It is fundamentally dishonest to call debt an asset. Meanwhile, many politicians align their actions with polls and election prospects. Regardless of whether their policies make sense or benefit citizens, politicians will implement them to their own, often personal, advantage. At best, it's to get re-elected. Looking at this from outside the fiat system makes it easier to see. Bitcoin supports the kind of constructive, critical debate that democracy depends on.

Bitcoin Fosters Independence

Bitcoin is independent of the fiat money system. It exists in parallel, in peaceful coexistence. If you find others who accept bitcoin, you don't need access to the old financial system at all. You become independent of it. The moment the existing system becomes hostile—or could become hostile—this independence is invaluable. I saw firsthand how a Canadian was unable to check into a hotel because his credit card had been frozen solely for making a small donation to truckers protesting COVID-19 measures. Refugees from Afghanistan and Ukraine have reported how they had to leave everything behind or have lost it along the way; everything except the private key to their bitcoin wallet. With a seed phrase in your head, all you're dependent on is your own memory. You are completely independent of the financial system.

The Bitcoin system itself is also independent: it has no central institution, no one controls it, and, thanks to

Satoshi Nakamoto's anonymity, there's no dependence on its creator(s). The profound decentralization of Bitcoin inherently creates independence from individual actors, regions, and cultures.

Starting from a value of zero and rising to around $100,000 per bitcoin by January 2025, Bitcoin's market value capitalization has grown to over $2 trillion. A number of early Bitcoiners who were smart enough to buy, securely store, and not sell their bitcoin have amassed significant wealth. A few have even become financially independent as a result. But financial independence starts much earlier than this; even if your holdings aren't enough to cover expenses for a lifetime, Bitcoin can still provide a degree of freedom. With just a small amount of wealth—say one bitcoin today—you could become independent of earned income for a time. It might even be enough to enable an extended sabbatical, get an additional degree, or simply give you the ability to walk away from an unbearable employer without having another job lined up first.[33]

New graduates receiving a bachelor's degree at age twenty-two who manage to acquire just half a bitcoin, or even less, have very likely secured their own retirement not only independent of the state pension system and the strength of their country's economy, but also of the global financial system. In about fifty years' time, half a bitcoin could not only cover one's own retirement, but perhaps also that of the next two generations. A single bitcoin today has the potential to provide economic independence for three or more generations.

Independence from a perpetually devaluing currency also frees you from the relentless pressure to invest money well enough to at least keep pace with inflation. It frees you from the additional chores of semi-professional investors who must concern themselves with stocks, real estate, bond markets, and related assets, just to generate a return above the future rate of inflation. With an inflation-proof currency like bitcoin, you are no longer beholden to financial market cycles, you're less tethered to the economy at large, and above all, you're less dependent on the politics that so heavily influence both.

Bitcoin does not belong to any one region. We don't know who developed it or where it was developed. Bitcoin is supranational, a global system independent of nation-states, making you independent of them, too, by owning bitcoin. Although regulations may vary by region, from a technical standpoint, Bitcoin is entirely beyond the control of individual countries. As long as there is access to the internet, Bitcoin will always work, and anyone can use it.

Bitcoin Leads to More Rational Decision-Making

A comedy-show line puts it this way: "We buy things we don't need with money we don't have to impress people we don't like."

That line, exaggerated though it is, aptly summarizes just how irrational many of our purchasing decisions can be. The goal is to prevent the economy from shrinking at almost any cost, given the fear of creating a self-reinforcing cycle of declining demand stemming from business failures and unemployment. At the same time, politicians risk losing elections if prosperity declines. So, demand is stimulated, almost regardless of the cost, just to keep the economy running. In such a system, saving is regarded as harmful because it reduces short-term demand. A high time preference, i.e., consuming today rather than tomorrow, is instilled into every individual.

Values like self-restraint, working, and saving before spending, carefully considering whether something is truly needed, modesty, and foresight have all become increasingly unimportant in many modern societies. The rational decision to forgo a dessert today, or even skip going out to a restaurant, so that you can afford a decent standard of living thirty years later in retirement, no longer makes sense if that money is going to be heavily devalued by then anyway. If, on the other hand, long-term saving makes it possible to afford not just one but several restaurant meals in the future, saving becomes a rational choice.

Rising prices tempt consumers to seek discounts. Yet discounted items are often cheaper because of their inferior quality. This leads to much shorter product lifespans. It is an irrational decision for manufacturers to produce refrigerators with a lifespan of ten years instead of twenty. It is equally an irrational decision for buyers to purchase such refrigerators only when they are 20% cheaper.

Money that remains stable in value enables long-term thinking. You begin to consider not just tomorrow or the day after, but the next generation and perhaps the one after that too. A long-term perspective underscores the value of better nutrition, a good relationship with your children, and a healthy planet. It is akin to the famous marshmallow test, pointing to long-term success, but not only for children.

Personal Responsibility, Independence, and Critical Thinking Pave the Way for a Smaller State

As a general rule, a privately spent euro is used more wisely and productively than a government euro. Of course, not always, but more often, private individuals tend to behave more rationally, whereas governments behave more irrationally. Politics is driven by the pursuit of votes, image, superficial persuasion, and, unfortunately, increasingly is driven by irrational and unreasonable decisions. The larger and more far-reaching a government's actions become, the less rational its decisions tend to be.

To avoid any misunderstandings, let me point out that we do need a government, and a strong one at that. Without one, we'd very quickly be at each other's throats. We need an authority that can take on tasks that, for one reason or another, a private individual cannot or will not handle. We need a structure that can provide at least a basic level of order and enforce a fair legal system, rather than one in which might makes right. A government whose aim is to improve life in society, and one that helps those who fall into hardship through no fault of their own.

During the COVID-19 crisis, government spending in Germany rose to more than 50% of gross domestic product. In other words, every second euro was spent by the government. This means the government received more of all goods and services produced in a given year than everyone else combined. That is very clearly too much. More personal responsibility naturally goes hand in hand with less government intervention. The state-planned economies of the collapsed socialist states of Eastern Europe vividly demonstrated how much a government's overreach reduced citizens' prosperity.[34]

In the long run, private decision-making outperforms short-term policies shaped by election cycles. Individual responsibility, in tandem with our daily challenges and personal circumstances, is far superior to any distant, bureaucratic action. A smaller state—one that steps back whenever tasks can be handled privately, or when an earlier intervention has achieved its desired effect and is no longer needed—would lead to far greater prosperity for society and its citizens as a whole. Switzerland provides an illustrative example of this.

Limited Access to Resources and Monetary Independence from the State Lead to a Smaller State

If an individual wants to afford more over the long term, s/he must either earn more or cut back elsewhere. For the vast majority, income can only be increased in the short term by working more. Those who cannot or do not want to work more must save.

Governments, however, are reluctant to implement spending cuts or tax increases because they are unpopular. The far easier, more convenient, and ultimately most tolerated path is through debt or simply *printing money*. Governments issue bonds, which are then bought by banks or the central bank. This process creates new money via the banking and financial system.

When unforeseen needs arise, such as the necessary expansion and rearmament of the German Armed Forces in response to the war in Ukraine, the government simply creates what it terms *special funds*. In truth, these are special debts, usually financed by bond issuance, which creates new money. This ability to simply conjure up money at will allows the state to finance ever more activities and keep endlessly expanding. In an inflationary monetary system, the government has virtually no economic limits. But in a non-inflationary system, the state would—just like individuals—have to decide how to generate more income, whether by raising taxes or, better still, by making real spending cuts elsewhere.

Bitcoin Brings Peace of Mind

The ability to take on greater personal responsibility, to honestly and critically recognize the good or bad around you, and above all, to have independence all bring peace of mind. It's easier to tolerate the nonsense that goes on in the world when you know you're not a defenseless victim of it. Independence sharpens your awareness of what's good, beautiful, and positive about the world. When the negatives affect you less, you can allow much more of the positives in.

This is just the spirit you encounter when you meet Bitcoiners. Yes, they are critical of an inflationary monetary system, but at the same time they are deeply positive about the opportunities that decentralization, honesty, and independence from central authorities can bring. They are part of a community that is based not on redistribution but on solidarity.

Ultimately, Bitcoin changes individuals first and, with time, could change society at large. Bitcoin fosters modesty, increased personal responsibility, independence, and the ability and courage to express one's own opinion. This strengthens democracy within a more limited but stronger government. And in the process, it could help to heal our battered planet.

Chapter 20:
A Better World?

The future is uncertain. We don't know what tomorrow will bring. Most of the time, nothing surprising happens, but every so often, something big comes along. The world is constantly changing, with innovation being one of the main drivers. More and more people are generating numerous ideas about what else could be done, inventing improvements to existing systems or rendering certain things obsolete altogether.

Disruptive innovation can change everything. Existing markets disappear, and new ones emerge. Successful companies fail while young startups grow into multibillion-dollar corporations within just a few years. All of our lives are constantly changing. If our great-grandparents had traveled through time to our current world, they would have found it bewildering and incomprehensible. Even now, some people struggle to understand the upcoming younger Generation Z.

Things that were taken for granted, that we once thought we could never live without, are disappearing.

The typewriters once found in every home and office were replaced by PCs, and PCs morphed into laptops and smartphones. The smartphone, like a black hole, is absorbing more and more into itself: the telephone, calendar, alarm clock, notepad, camera, wallet, bank account, newspaper personal ads, maps, navigation, and much more.

The challenge with disruptive innovations is twofold. First, we often fail to recognize them. Worse still, when they emerge, we dismiss them as nonsense because we don't understand them. They don't fit into our established worldview, especially as they're meant to fundamentally change or even destroy it. We struggle to grasp disruptive innovations because we are too attached to our existing views and habits, as well as to our self-confidence and identity within the familiar. And when we don't understand these radically new things, we can automatically develop a bad feeling about them and reject them, which culminates in the common knee-jerk reaction of *What nonsense.*

Yet it is precisely this often unconscious reaction that marks something radically new. The art, of course, lies in distinguishing real nonsense from perceived nonsense that is, in fact, disruptive innovation.

Even after seventeen years, the overwhelming majority, especially the experts in the existing fiat system, still regard Bitcoin as nonsense. Hardly any established central bankers, economists, or politicians can recognize the potential of Bitcoin. Doing so would automatically mean the complete devaluation of their accumulated knowledge, their careers, their worldview, and ultimately their professional identity.

Our capacity for innovation declines with age. Almost all major mathematical breakthroughs were made by people in their twenties. In contrast, virtually all the top positions in politics, business, and especially at central banks are held by people over fifty, and in some cases, much older.

This makes disruptive innovations doubly difficult for us to recognize. They clash with our worldview, and moreover, the key decision-makers are far too old to embrace them. A third factor compounds the problem: disruptive innovations often fail and are generally slow to catch on initially. This means only a small number of early adopters try out radically new things.

At the beginning, many innovations are still immature; they function incorrectly, aren't user-friendly, and the new ecosystems they require may not yet exist but are emerging gradually. These teething problems seem to confirm that they're *nonsense*. Consider the early days of computers. They had extremely limited usability, and, by and large, the general public considered them nonsense. There were virtually no programs, and the few that did exist could do very little, plus hardly anyone—at least not the general public—knew how to operate one. Suddenly, with the advent of the smartphone, everyone was carrying a high-performance computer in their pocket.

Disruptive innovations have a delayed effect, developing exponentially only when a critical mass of users has been reached. The problem is that if you fail to recognize them until after this threshold has been crossed, it's already too late. The momentum then becomes so powerful that two things happen. Disruptive innovations become unstoppable, spreading at lightning speed, and almost all the players in the old world cannot adapt, which eventually forces them to go under.

Bitcoin has all the hallmarks of becoming one of the most disruptive innovations of our time, thanks to its defining features—decentralization and lack of control by any individual or small group, its hard cap of 21 million and resulting immunity to dilution, and its abilities to uniquely define a digital good, to be divided infinitely, and to be transferred worldwide at very high speed and virtually no cost. There has never been anything like it in human history. Never before has there been a fully transparent and honest currency. Never before has it been possible to exercise full personal control over your money while also being able to transfer it in any amount, anywhere in the world, around the clock, quickly and inexpensively. And never before have billions of people currently excluded from the financial system had the opportunity to participate in global banking with nothing more than a smartphone and an internet connection.

Our sovereignties, regardless of their form of government, are currently operating on the premise of a permanently expanding money supply. With only a few exceptions, highly decorated politicians, central bankers, economists, and Nobel laureates are deeply convinced that inflation enables a healthy economy, provided that it's kept under control. In their view, a non-inflating money supply, and Bitcoin in particular, would lead to economic and social collapse. That is why they dismiss Bitcoin as nonsense—ironically, a very good indicator of Bitcoin's disruptive potential.

The transition to a sound monetary system can happen gradually and positively, or abruptly and painfully. In the gradual case, an existing system is gradually supplemented and, perhaps eventually, replaced, with limited disruption. The internet, as a parallel medium, has gradually been replacing traditional media over the past thirty years. Many media outlets have integrated it, reinvented themselves through it, and developed new offerings. Others are failing. Similarly, fiat currencies could integrate bitcoin, thereby strengthening it.

Inflation and the collapse of financial systems have repeatedly served as catalysts for major social crises. The Western Roman Empire fell in AD 440 after the value of its currency was steadily debased. Before the French Revolution, there was a period of rampant inflation. Germany's hyperinflation of 1923 was followed by Hitler's initially failed violent coup, which unfortunately did succeed ten years later.

A sound financial system, one that does not quietly dispossess the weakest members of society through the back door of inflation, is a prerequisite for peaceful and productive coexistence. Bitcoin could well be what prevents deeper social conflict, provided the transition occurs peacefully.

As with a drug addict, however, the withdrawal process could be both painful and unpleasant. With drugs, even if withdrawal is successful, life afterward is not better in every aspect than it was during the addiction. With no drugs, there is no high. There is no euphoria, no sense of invincibility. Without drugs, life is marked by fewer extremes. Some who have made it even describe it as boring.

Just as backing the dollar with gold once disciplined and stabilized the monetary system, bitcoin can also mitigate or prevent the adverse effects of perpetual monetary expansion. The more stable the money, the more stable and successful the society that uses it.

This is just what bitcoin will help to achieve.

Chapter 21:
The Community

Hardly anyone manages to understand Bitcoin without some assistance from others. As already discussed, Bitcoin is a disruptive innovation that doesn't fit into our established worldview. At first, it's difficult to grasp. A database that's distributed and can't be controlled by anyone; a database where adding new records requires a great deal of effort; the resulting currency capped at 21 million units; a digital good that can't be copied? Nothing like it has ever existed before.

Bitcoin is the result of a decades-long process of failed attempts similar to it. Why should it have succeeded this time? Bitcoin is not intuitive. Most people need time and help to understand it.

It is often the repeated nudges of others that eventually kick-start the discovery process. It takes curiosity and openness. A healthy dose of skepticism toward the established financial system helps in appreciating bitcoin's non-inflationary design. The sometimes extreme price fluctuations

become easier to endure with a long-term perspective and some short-term resilience.

Bitcoin exposes the weaknesses of the financial system. But unlike other critics, it doesn't stop there. Bitcoin offers a constructive way forward. When Bitcoiners meet, there's little to no complaining at all about how bad things are. Instead, you hear opinions, discussions, and ideas that revolve around how to spread Bitcoin further and make it more useful. Bitcoiners do not dwell on the past or present in a negative way. They look constructively to the future.

The essence of Bitcoin is apolitical—neither left, nor right, nor anywhere else for that matter. The system simply continues, independent of its creators, their origins, or their political views. We will probably never know who developed Bitcoin. What we do know is that the community as a whole advances it through ever more add-on developments and growing adoption. *We are all Satoshi* describes this. It's all of us, as a community, who drive the continuous development of Bitcoin.

This is the spirit of the Bitcoin community: critical, open to new things, and constructively forward-thinking with a long-term perspective. Focused on finding and developing solutions instead of complaining. Apolitical. Stress-resistant, kind, and very honest. And Bitcoiners come from all walks of life—many IT professionals, but also tradespeople, warehouse workers, salespeople, business and economics experts, a few politicians, entrepreneurs, free spirits, architects, professors, and many more. The youngest aren't even old enough to vote, while others I've met are well into their eighties.

Since 2021, a highly diverse community has taken shape in Germany, Europe, and worldwide. Take, for example, *Einundzwanzig* (Twenty-One); due to bitcoin's 21 million cap, the number 21 has become symbolic among Bitcoiners. In the German-speaking world, since launching the podcast in 2019, the *Einundzwanzig* community has expanded to include a range of activities, including the podcast, regional meetups (236 monthly meetups as of October 2024), and various events. There's a shop where you can buy various bitcoin-related merchandise, and even a Swiss-based association that supports various activities through donations. Just as Bitcoin has no central leader, the community is also decentralized. Ideas are simply put into practice, with tremendous energy and love poured into podcasts, memes, and events. Throughout these years, I've never encountered a single unpleasant or dishonest Bitcoiner. If there were room for improvement, it would be in the ratio of women involved: although it's growing, this number is still far too small.

In the German-speaking world, you'll find *Blocktrainer*, which is Europe's largest Bitcoin-only YouTube channel, and there are many podcasts as well (*Nodesignal, Münzweg, Was Bitcoin bringt, Bitcoin verstehen,* and many more). Numerous companies produce or sell bitcoin merchandise, from the BitBox02 hardware wallet to Bitcoin-branded wine. In Plochingen, a city south of Stuttgart, Germany, there's even a Bitcoin hotel. There's also Aprycot Media, which publishes Bitcoin books, mainly translations of

English-language works. Major events of high merit are organized by Volksbank Bayern Mitte, the Kuchar brothers in Prague, and the Einundzwanzig community, including its *Zitadelle* conference. Bitcoiners meet up in Mallorca or go sailing together off the coast of Croatia in the Mediterranean. Some go skiing together or might be found meditating in an old church. The *Bitcoin im Bundestag* initiative offers members of the German parliament and their staff the opportunity to learn about and gain access to Bitcoin.

In November 2022, while I was in the hospital for a few days, I tweeted about our upcoming trip to Madeira. Almost immediately, Jürgen, a Bitcoiner who has been living there for some time, contacted me. We arranged to meet and got together at an expat gathering. Within a single day, we knew everyone we needed to know in Madeira: a real estate agent, other expats, an angel investor, the operator of a startup center, and plenty of other wonderful people besides. Jürgen later even connected me with the CEO of the investment arm of the King of Bhutan.

Even more valuable than Bitcoin itself is the community that has emerged around it. Once one understands Bitcoin, it can feel almost boring because it merely changes. Certainly, you can delve into the technology, but you dive even deeper into the community. Bitcoin is not just about numbers and price values; it's about people, ideas, and inspiration. The community looks toward the future rather than getting stuck on present problems. Voluntary engagement, creative ideas on how bitcoin can create value, or how it might solve challenges, or at least contribute to their solutions—these are the things that characterize the Bitcoin community.

On January 15, 2011—at a time when bitcoin's price was still under $1—Hal Finney, the developer who had created some of the foundational technologies that preceded Bitcoin and had corresponded closely with Satoshi Nakamoto, summed up the potential impact on society of Bitcoin and its community. For him, Bitcoin and its community were about creating a positive impact on society:

> *Since we're all rich with Bitcoin or will be once they're worth a million dollars like everyone expects, we ought to put some of this unearned wealth to good use.*

Conclusion: Bitcoin Is Honesty

Bitcoin is many things, and it means something different to everyone.

For me, Bitcoin is honesty. The system is open and transparent. The software that runs the Bitcoin network can be inspected down to the smallest detail. Open source means that every line of code is publicly available. All of its mechanisms, especially the algorithm that limits the number of bitcoin to 21 million, are transparent for everyone to see. There are no secret functions, no hidden agenda, and no tricks or traps. Even the intentions of its creator(s) are laid out openly and clearly in the white paper.

Because no individual, group, or even government has direct control over the system, selfish, irrational, and illogical behavior is excluded. There is no room for dishonesty.

We humans are not always honest. Whether intentionally or unintentionally, we often express ourselves in ways that mislead, perhaps to achieve certain goals. We sugarcoat, highlight some aspects over others, omit important information, present information in a distorted context,

or tell outright falsehoods. There are countless shades of *truth*, from a slightly exaggerated compliment to schemes built on outright lies. Depending on the intention and outcome, we must distinguish among good lies, white lies, mistakes, and socially acceptable lies. Is an excuse also a lie? And how often are we tempted to make certain claims when we know that they can't be verified? *The traffic was awful, that's why I'm late.* Was there really a traffic jam? If not, is it a lie? It could be true. After all, it could happen to anyone, probably already has. A socially acceptable lie. It's fine.

There are different estimates as to how often we lie. According to an article in the Neue Zürcher Zeitung by Ms. Ludewig, the number is approximately 25 times. Per day.[35]

Campaign promises, corporate strategy announcements, explanations of inflation—all topics that, as they are presented, rarely match reality.

Calling money stable when its value halves over thirty-five years, which corresponds to 2% annual inflation, is an obvious untruth, even a lie. Yet a lie that has been so widely accepted, supposedly on scientific grounds, that it's no longer questioned. Is an accepted lie still counted as a lie? Massive debt programs are referred to as assets, so-called special funds. Yet when we spend 100 billion on the German Armed Forces, the debt increases. No asset is created in any shape or form. In his 2022 Christmas lecture, Professor Hans-Werner Sinn listed and totaled these *special funds*. The total was approximately 1.7 trillion.

The truth can be unpleasant. Maybe even dangerous: it could threaten our very social order. A quote often attributed to Henry Ford puts it like this:

> *It is well enough that people of the nation do not understand our banking and monetary system, for if they did, I believe there would be a revolution before tomorrow morning.*

We certainly don't want to start a revolution. From this perspective, the lies surrounding the monetary system and inflation may even be justifiable, socially acceptable white lies. They are nonetheless wrong: lies that lead to misjudgments, declining prosperity, inequality, social division, and worse.

Honesty entails respecting others, and Bitcoin respects both individuals and society; it has no agenda. The world can rely on Bitcoin. It doesn't sugarcoat anything: the price of bitcoin, measured in traditional fiat currencies, is still highly volatile. That volatility can cause you stress or even financial loss if you sell bitcoin at the wrong time.

The dishonest fiat system trains us to be dishonest people. Bitcoin shows us, and will show even more clearly in the future, that an honest society is a far better one. The adage "honesty is the best policy" reminds us that truth leads to lasting success. A lie may bring success in the short term, but it never lasts.

Bitcoin's honesty is the foundation of its growing acceptance, its network effects, its wealth effects, and its expanding technology platform with ever more applications.

Bitcoin's honesty is a unique, enduring, and virtually unmatched competitive advantage over inflationary fiat systems. This honesty is what guarantees Bitcoin's success. It points the way toward a better, healthier, and more humane society and world.

Bitcoin Quotes

Satoshi Nakamoto

It might make sense just to get some in case it catches on.

I'm sure that in twenty years there will either be very large transaction volume or no volume.

The root problem with conventional currency is all the trust that's required to make it work. The central bank must be trusted not to debase the currency, but the history of fiat currencies is full of breaches of that trust.

Michael Saylor

Bitcoin is a bank in cyberspace, run by incorruptible software, offering a global, affordable, simple and secure savings account to billions of people that don't have the option or desire to run their own hedge fund.

There is no second best.

Hal Finney

Bitcoin is an amazing cryptographic achievement, and the ability to create something that is not duplicable in the digital world has enormous value.

Jeff Booth

Everything goes to zero against Bitcoin.

A 13-year-old girl

Papa, why isn't more money printed for kids who are poor or sick?

About the Author

Dr. Alex von Frankenberg is an author and technology expert who has played a defining role in shaping Europe's and Germany's startup ecosystem. For two decades, he led High-Tech Gründerfonds (HTGF), an early-stage seed fund, building it into Europe's most active early-stage investor with more than 800 seed investments and €2 billion under management.

Before HTGF, Alex worked at Siemens Research, in strategy and IT consulting, and helped build both a startup and a company builder, experiences that gave him a deep understanding of how innovation takes root and scales.

He earned his MBA from the University of Texas at Austin and his Ph.D. from the University of Mannheim, where his dissertation on *de facto* technology standards foreshadowed his lifelong fascination with network effects and disruptive innovation.

That fascination eventually led him to Bitcoin, which he views as a breakthrough capable of becoming the *de facto* standard for a store of value—*honest money* for the digital age.

You can reach Alex at hodltrainer@gmail.com or on X (formerly Twitter) at @Justdoitalex.

Endnotes

[1] Statista, "Gross Domestic Product (GDP) of Germany from 1991 to 2024," https://de.statista.com.

[2] BitDegree, "What Is the Cantillon Effect?," https://www.bitdegree.org/crypto/learn/crypto-terms/what-is-the-cantillon-effect.

[3] Statista, "Development of the M2 Money Supply in the Euro Area," https://de.statista.com/statistik/daten/studie/241824/umfrage/entwicklung-der-geldmenge-m2-in-der-euro-zone/.

[4] Adam Fergusson, *When Money Dies: The Nightmare of Deficit Spending, Devaluation, and Hyperinflation in Weimar Germany* (New York: PublicAffairs, 2010), Kindle edition.

[5] Ernst Wolff, "Ernsthafte Bedrohung des Geldwerts," *Think Beyond the Obvious*, https://think-beyondtheobvious.com/ernsthafte-bedrohung-des-geldwerts/.

[6] U.S. Department of the Treasury, "National Deficit by Year," *Fiscal Data*, https://fiscaldata.treasury.gov/americas-finance-guide/national-deficit/#us-deficit-by-year.

[7] Encyclopaedia Britannica, s.v. "Fiat Money," https://www.britannica.com/topic/fiat-money.

[8] Statista, "Number of Violations of the Stability Criteria by Eurozone Countries," https://de.statista.com/statistik/daten/studie/200068/umfrage/anzahl-der-verstoesse-der-eurolaender-gegen-diestabilitaetskriterien-der-eurozone/.

[9] CompaniesMarketCap, "Gold Market Capitalization," October 2025, https://companiesmarketcap.com/assets-by-market-cap/.

[10] *Oeconomia*, documentary film, directed by Carmen Losmann (Germany: Peter Hartwig Filmproduktion, 2020), https://www.3sat.de/film/dokumentarfilm/oeconomia-100.html.

[11] Jesse Colombo, "Will Deutsche Bank Survive This Wave of Trouble?," *Investing.com*, May 2016, https://www.investing.com/analysis/may-2016:-will-deutsche-bank-survive-this-wave-of-trouble-or-will-it-be-200131715; Tyler Durden, "Deutsche Bank Extends Losses Near Record Lows," *ZeroHedge*, September 19, 2016, https://www.zerohedge.com/news/2016-09-19/deutsche-bank-extends-losses-near-record-lows-significantly-undercapitalzied-even-wi.

[12] Knut Blind, *Standardization Processes of New Technologies: Conditions and Corporate Strategies in the Establishment of Product Technologies as De Facto Standards* (Mannheim: University of Mannheim, 1997).

[13] Satoshi Nakamoto Institute, "Micropayments," https://satoshi.nakamotoinstitute.org/quotes/micropayments/.

[14] Gold.de, "Goldreserven weltweit," https://www.gold.de/goldreserven/.

[15] *Neue Zürcher Zeitung*, "Volksinitiative will Nationalbank zum Kauf von Bitcoin verpflichten," https://www.nzz.ch/wirtschaft/nun-kommt-die-volksinitiative-welche-die-nationalbank-zum-kauf-von-bitcoin-verpflichten-will-ld.1827256.

[16] Blockworks, "Bhutan's Investment Fund Is Mining Bitcoin," https://blockworks.co/news/bhutan-investment-fund-crypto.

[17] Wikipedia contributors, "Gold Standard," *Wikipedia*, https://de.wikipedia.org/wiki/Goldstandard; "What Happened in 1971," https://www.wtfhappenedin1971.com.

[18] Statista, "Currency Reserves of the Swiss National Bank," https://de.statista.com/statistik/daten/studie/424953/umfrage/waehrungsreserven-der-schweizerischen-nationalbank/.

[19] Tyler Durden, "Saudi Central Bank Caught Secretly Buying 160 Tonnes of Gold," *ZeroHedge*, https://www.zerohedge.com/commodities/saudi-central-bank-caught-secretly-buying-160-tonnes-gold-switzerland.

[20] Isabel Schnabel, interview, YouTube video, https://www.youtube.com/watch?v=ghlScsDl030.

[21] Calculation based on a fixed supply of 21 million bitcoin divided by an estimated global population of eight billion.

[22] Wikipedia contributors, "Goldverbot," *Wikipedia*, https://de.wikipedia.org/wiki/Goldverbot.

[23] Central Intelligence Agency, *The World Factbook*, https://relief.unboundmedicine.com/relief/view/The-World-Factbook/563280/all/World.

[24] Bitnodes, "Bitcoin Network Nodes," https://bitnodes.io.

[25] Jonathan Bier, *The Blocksize War: The Battle Over Who Controls Bitcoin's Protocol* (Independently published, 2021).

[26] Börse.de, "Geldmenge M2 in den USA," https://www.boerse.de/staatsverschuldung/geldmenge-m2-usa-in-mrd-usd.

[27] Alex Gladstein, post on X (formerly Twitter), December 2023, https://x.com/Justdoitalex/status/1731221378580242749.

[28] Chainalysis, *Crypto Crime Report 2024*, https://go.chainalysis.com/crypto-crime-2024.html.

[29] Benjamin Wallace-Wells, "Gary Gensler on SBF and the Crypto Crackdown," *New York Magazine*, February 2023, https://nymag.com/intelligencer/2023/02/gary-gensler-on-meeting-with-sbf-and-his-crypto-crackdown.html.

[30] Interview video, YouTube, https://www.youtube.com/watch?v=0czPdSF7tXE; LinkedIn post, https://www.linkedin.com/feed/update/urn:li:activity:7033354090847850496/.

[31] EnBW, "Warum Windräder stillstehen," https://www.enbw.com/unternehmen/themen/windkraft/warum-windraeder-stillstehen.html; *Merkur*, "Rekord-Entschädigungen für ungenutzten Strom," https://www.merkur.de/wirtschaft/erneuerbare-energien-rekord-entschaedigungen-strom-ungenutzt-windkraft-teurer-zr-91974023.html.

[32] Coinpages, "Was ist Coinpages?," https://coinpages.io/coinpages-news/.

[33] Marc Steiner, *Bitcoins verwahren und vererben: Ein praktischer Ratgeber* (Aprycot Media, 2020).

[34] Bundeszentrale für politische Bildung (bpb), "Entwicklung der öffentlichen Finanzen," August 8, 2024, https://www.bpb.de/kurz-knapp/zahlen-und-fakten/soziale-situation-in-deutschland/61867/entwicklung-der-oeffentliche-finanzen/.

[35] *Neue Zürcher Zeitung*, "Durchschnittlich lügt jeder 25 Mal am Tag," https://www.nzz.ch/panorama/durchschnittlich-luegt-jeder-25-mal-am-tag-ld.1442957.

www.ingramcontent.com/pod-product-compliance
Lightning Source LLC
LaVergne TN
LVHW090321210926
848480LV00001B/320